The Odd Squad's SEXY SEX MANUAL

by Allan and Becky Plenderleith

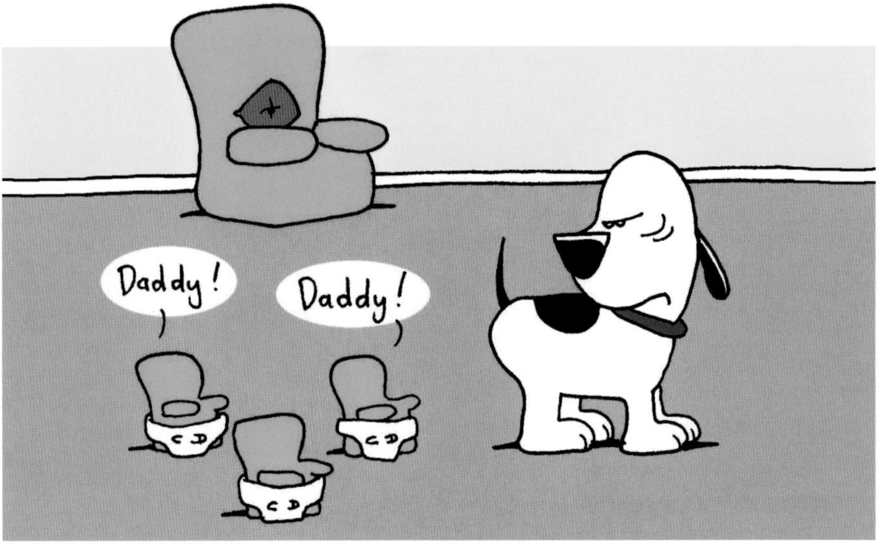
Daddy!
Daddy!

RAVETTE PUBLISHING

THE ODD SQUAD and all related characters © 2004
Created by Allan Plenderleith

First published in 2004 by
Ravette Publishing Limited
Unit 3, Tristar Centre
Star Road, Partridge Green
West Sussex RH13 8RA

Printed in Belgium by Proost ISBN: 1 84161 220 0

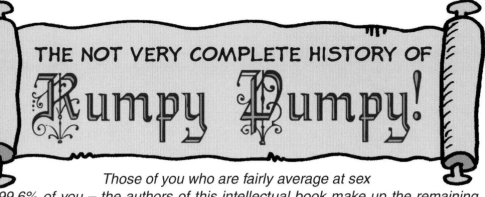

THE NOT VERY COMPLETE HISTORY OF Rumpy Pumpy!

Those of you who are fairly average at sex (99.6% of you – the authors of this intellectual book make up the remaining percentage) will be thinking "But surely sex between man and woman, or man and sheep hasn't changed since time began?" In out, in out, shake it all about? Correct, smartarse. But here's some info just discovered in the world's fave history book, the Bible, hidden inside the back sleeve cover…

NEANDERTHAL MAN

It's amazing that the human race didn't die out there and then… the women were so repulsively hairy, and smelly. Mr. Ug only had sex with yeti-like Mrs. Ug when he realised he needed an heir to inherit his bloody club, instead preferring to get jiggy the rest of the time with Mr. Mammoth who was a lot less hairy than her.

AAH! THAT WAS AMAZING!
IF ONLY WE HAD INVENTED FIRE. I'D LOVE A CIGARETTE.

THE EGYPTIANS

It's only half full !!
Oh, come on! I'm only human!!

That Cleopatra was a kinky little madam (that wasn't ass's milk she liked t bathe in). In fact, Cleopatra wasn't lusted after for her beauty (she was actuall a minger who wore way too much eye make-up), but because it was rumoure that she had several breasts. That's why pyramids are always found in cluster of 3 or more – they're a homage to her fantastic abnormality. Another thing mummification wasn't about a passage to the next life, it's a result of bondag games gone wrong – they forgot to cut breathing holes.

THE ROMANS

These dress-wearing guys are famous for invading the rest of the world. But this is in fact a cover-up, a spin doctoring stunt by the Labour party. What they are actually famous for invading doesn't bear thinking about. Well, all right then, suffice to say, the Coliseum is, in fact, a mispronunciation of "Colon-see-' em". Say no more (skirts = easy access!).

Bend over, boy or it's the lions for you!
I'll take the lions!! The lions!

THE VIKINGS

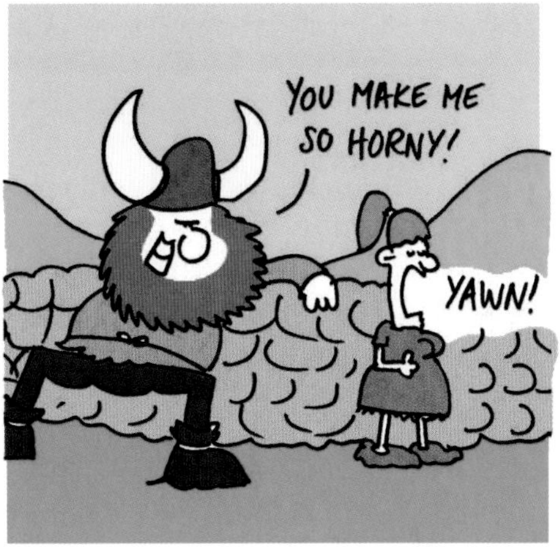
YOU MAKE ME SO HORNY!
YAWN!

Ooh, imagine being cooped up on a longboat for weeks on end with all those hot, rippling and sweaty torsos. B.O. No wonder then, that as soon as they arrived, they went on a desperate rampage looking for power showers and jacuzzis. Only then could the Vikings begin practising their dodgy European chat-up techniques on the British girls - the most notoriously difficult girls in the world to impress with cheesy lines.

THE ELIZABETHANS

Yes, it is true that Sir Walter Raleigh did introduce the potato to Britain (not including N. Ireland). But he didn't bring it back from America, he found it growing in the moist and fertile nether regions of the not particularly hygienic Mrs. Raleigh.

As for the tobacco? Well, Mrs. Raleigh also had a terribly hairy upper lip. Hmm, what a honey. No wonder Sir Raleigh wanted to be an explorer. Alas Sir Walt never went further than the port at Southampton – terrible seasickness, you see.

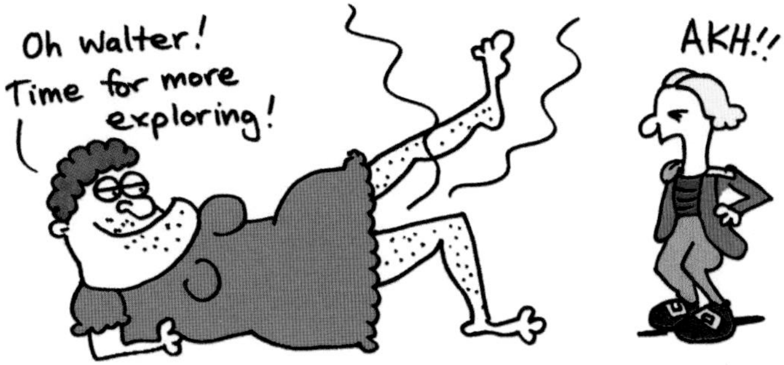
Oh Walter! Time for more exploring!
AKH!!

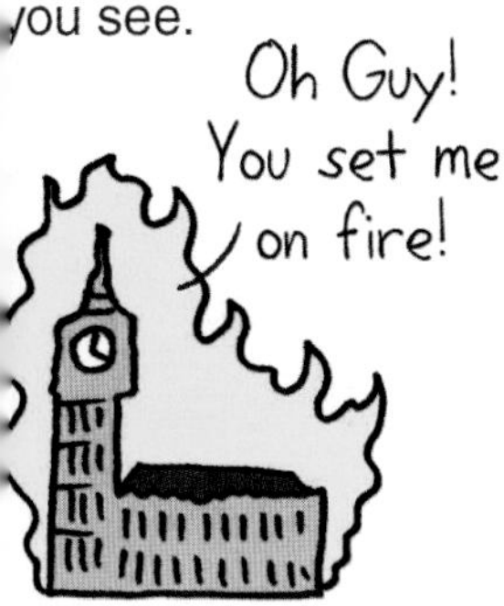
Oh Guy! You set me on fire!

PS: In 1605 it is widely believed that Guy Fawkes tried to blow up the Houses of Parliament. Panty-crap! Firstly, the fire started because he was shagging the Prime Minister's secretary in the basement and the friction caused by his condom, made from sheep's intestines, caused lots of sparks which started the fire. Secondly, "Fawkes" is a mispronunciation of his name by posh people.

THE INDUSTRIAL AGE

This was when the first steam-powered vibrator was invented. What more do you need to know?

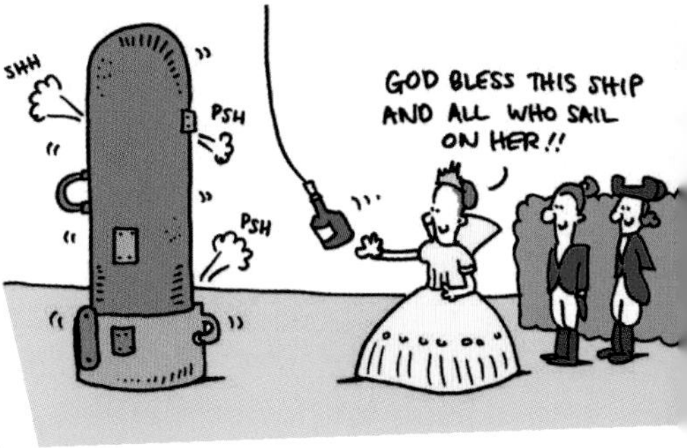
SHH
PSH
PSH
GOD BLESS THIS SHIP AND ALL WHO SAIL ON HER!!

THE VICTORIANS

This sex age is characterised by child chimney sweeps. It's little known that child chimney sweeps *only* cleaned chimneys on their day off to earn extra money to buy sherbet dips. Their full-time job was to sweep the vaginas of frigid Victorian women, notably from the middle and upper classes.

Indeed, little Jason Stewart was the most famous chimney sweep of all, having been hired to give Queen Victoria a thorough sweeping on her 73rd birthday. He was never seen again. Child chimney sweeps weren't black from soot you know…

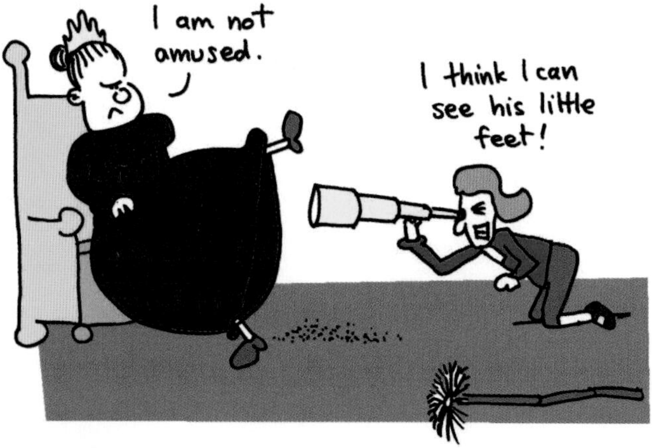
I am not amused.
I think I can see his little feet!

THE INTERNETIANS

Like the Ice Age all over again. Our internet age will become extinct as physical procreation is actually taken over by virtual sex. Hey, but at least we'll all die happy.

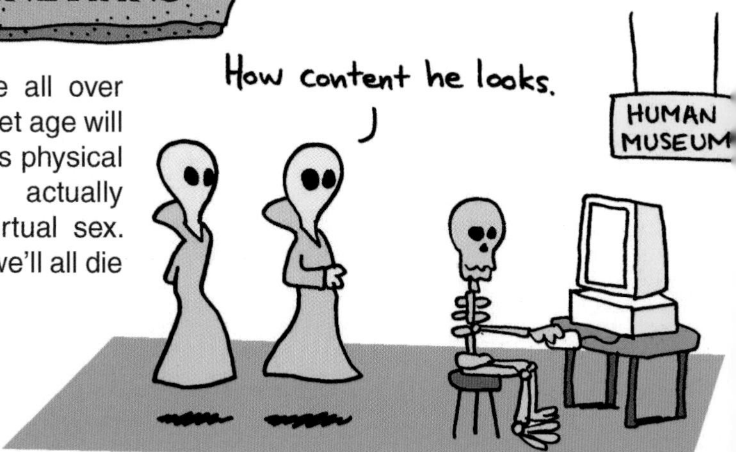
How content he looks.
HUMAN MUSEUM

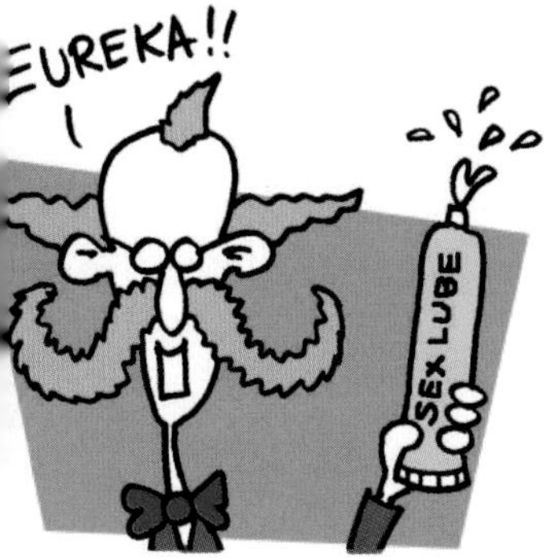
EUREKA!!
SEX LUBE

GREAT SEX INVENTIONS!

The invention of the wheel? The television? Pacemaker? Pah. Hardly life-enhancing are they?!! These are the inventions we are forever indebted to.

6000 B.C. : BEER

Created by the Babylonians. Possibly the best invention in the world. Well, have you seen Babylonian women?! Euch!!

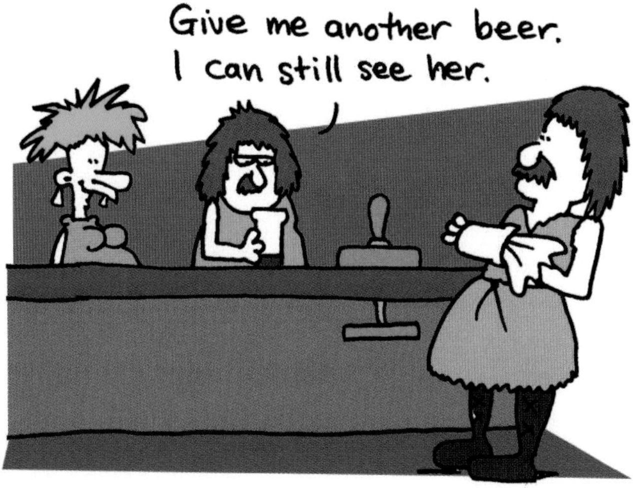
Give me another beer. I can still see her.

1ST CENTURY A.D. : THE COMPASS

The first compass was invented by the Chinese to help man find his way round a woman's body. Men are still learning to use it though.

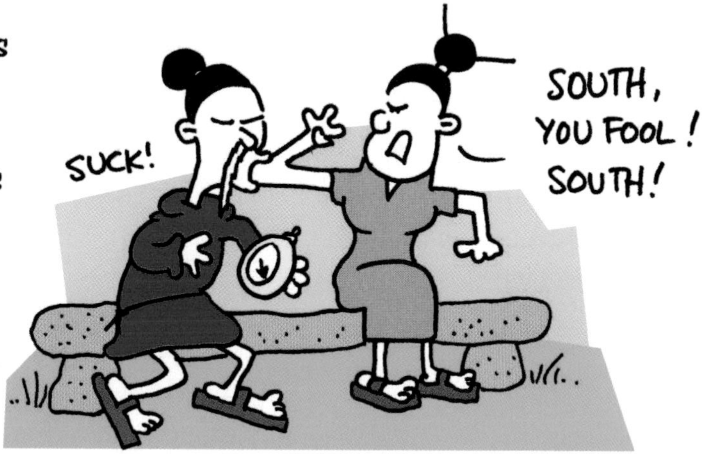
SUCK!
SOUTH, YOU FOOL! SOUTH!

1596: FIRST FLUSHING TOILET

Invented by Sir John Harrington, not for getting rid of floaters as is commonly thought, but so that couples can flush away their soggy condoms and kill innocent dolphins in the sea.

COUGH! CHOKE!

STOP SWALLOWING WE CAN USE THAT

1840: STAMPS

Sir Rowland Hill invented stamps to help men and women perfect their licking technique, and get them used to a foul taste.

UGH, SECOND CLASS...

1845: RUBBER BAND

Stephen Perry was a male strippergram working in Marie Antoinette's royal court. He invented the rubber band as a flesh-coloured cock ring to help him keep working through the long, degrading nights.

OFF WITH HIS HEAD!

847: RING-SHAPED DONUT

Hanson Crockett Gregory created this doughy delight because he couldn't get a real girlfriend, plus, you could eat this sex aid afterwards too!

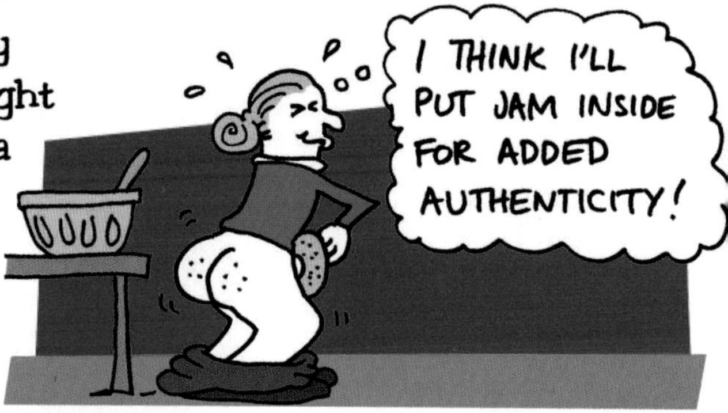
I THINK I'LL PUT JAM INSIDE FOR ADDED AUTHENTICITY!

870: CHEWING GUM

Created by Thomas Adams to help disguise the foul taste left by oral sex, and in many cases, just kissing.

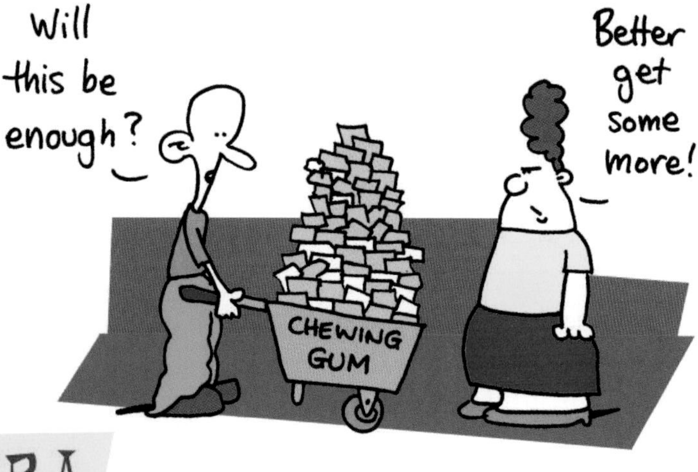
Will this be enough?
CHEWING GUM
Better get some more!

888: CAMERA

George Eastmen invented the camera to snap some "sexy pics" of his fatso wife, knowing full well that the camera would never lie and the truth would force her into finally going on a diet.

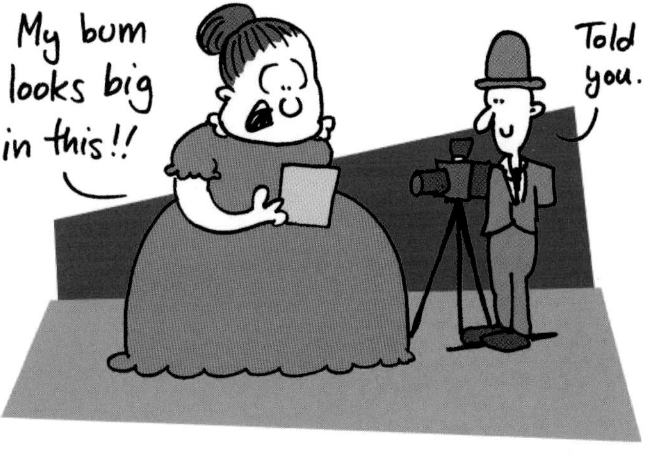
My bum looks big in this!!
Told you.

1897: ASPIRIN

Felix Hoffman invented the aspirin after he woke up without his beer goggles to find he'd just had a drunken one-night stand with minger Queen Victoria.

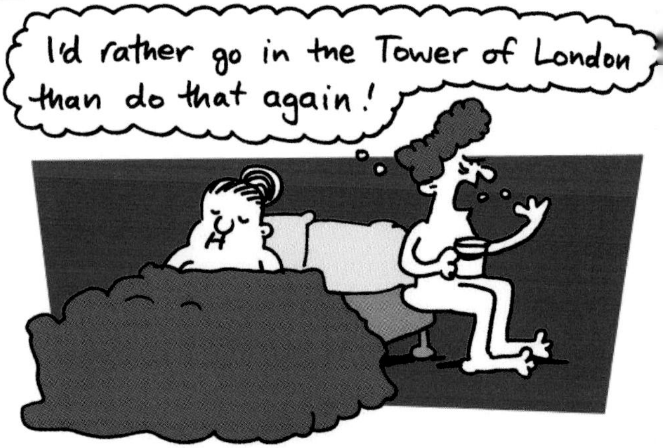
I'd rather go in the Tower of London than do that again!

1913: BRA

A cunning ruse created by Mary Phelps Jacob, because the difficulty men experience in removing the bra, often puts them off sex completely.

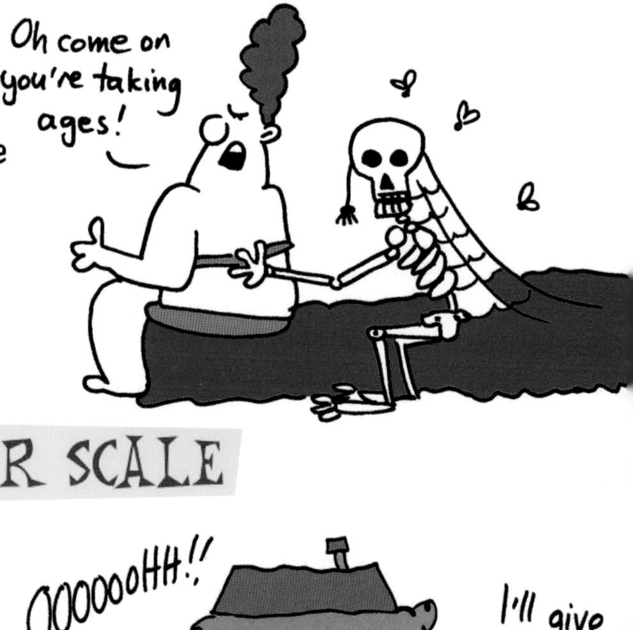
Oh come on you're taking ages!

1935: RICHTER SCALE

Charles Richter and Beno Gutenburg invented this earth-tremoring scale to see how rampant their sex session had been.

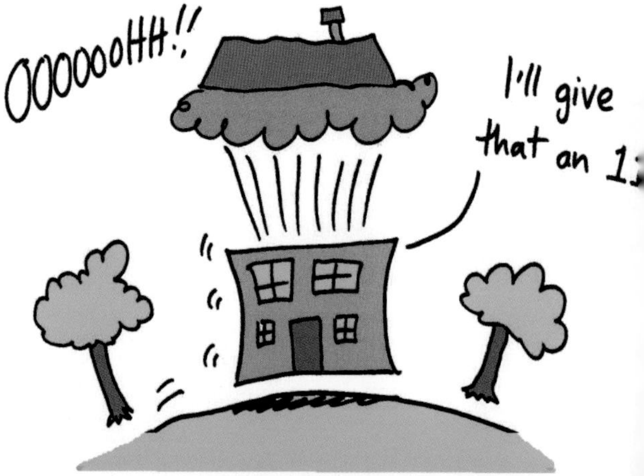
OOOOOOHH!!
I'll give that an 1

940: GAS POWERED LAWN MOWER

Leonard Goodall created the lawn mower because his wife insisted he cut the grass before she would have sex with him. A practise which still takes place to this day.

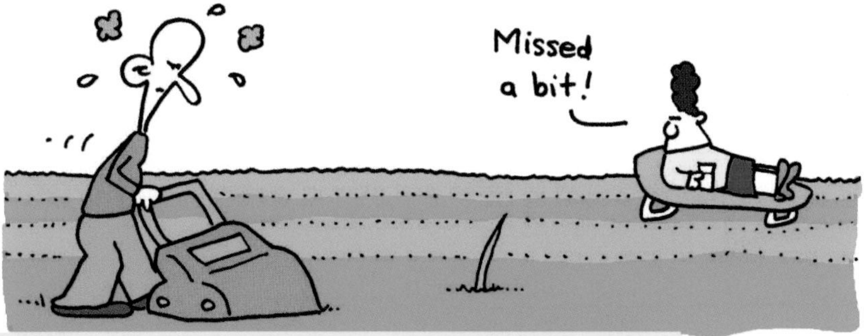
Missed a bit!

950: TV REMOTE CONTROL

Robert Adler invented this gadget to help women flick the TV during sex.

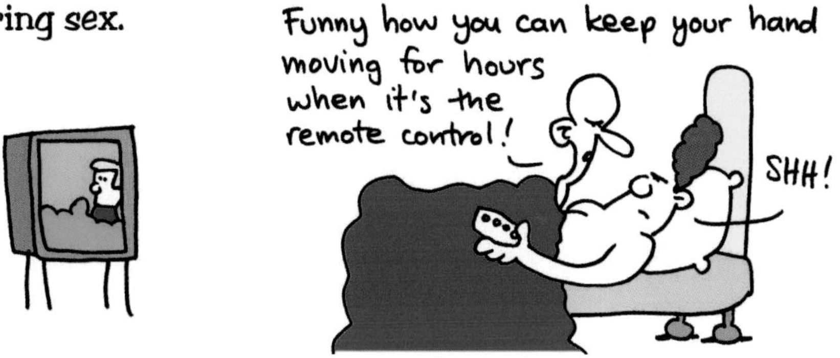
Funny how you can keep your hand moving for hours when it's the remote control!
SHH!

940: WHITE CORRECTION FLUID

Shrewdly invented by Bette Nesmith to con her husband into thinking he had already come. He fell for it every time; they never had children.

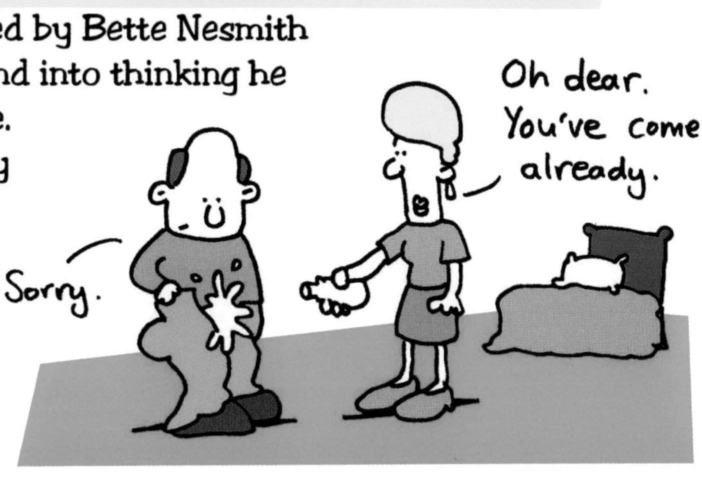
Oh dear. You've come already.
Sorry.

SEX IN THE ARTS

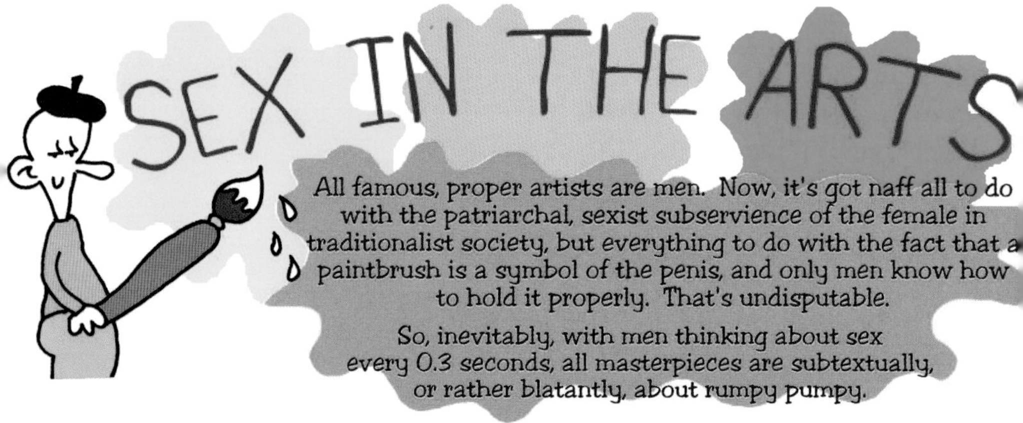

All famous, proper artists are men. Now, it's got naff all to do with the patriarchal, sexist subservience of the female in traditionalist society, but everything to do with the fact that a paintbrush is a symbol of the penis, and only men know how to hold it properly. That's undisputable.

So, inevitably, with men thinking about sex every 0.3 seconds, all masterpieces are subtextually, or rather blatantly, about rumpy pumpy.

CAVEMEN ART

What's a caveman to do in the short hours between the mutilation of mammoths and hairy cavewoman cruising?! The TV's full of repeats: Top of the Rocks, Eatelders, 15 to 1.......all dinosaurs! Why, imaginatively create graffiti using their very own semen, that's what.

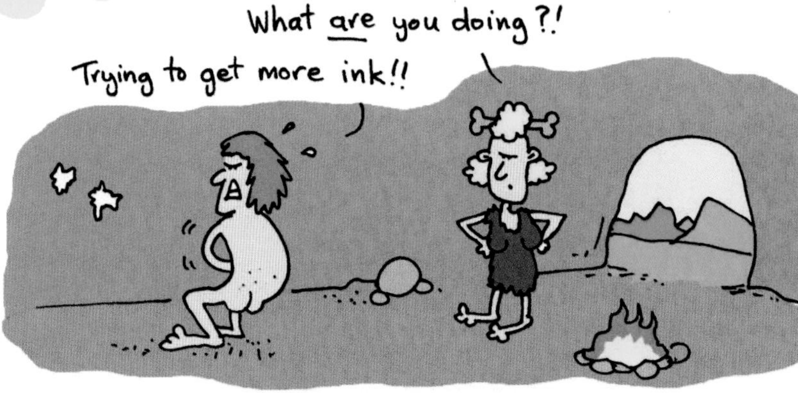
Trying to get more ink!!
What are you doing?!

The GIRL with the PEARL EARRING

It should have been a whole necklace but Vermeer's Shitsu started doing a skid on his newly-imported chequerboard disco floor and put Vermeer off. No wonder she looks so relieved.

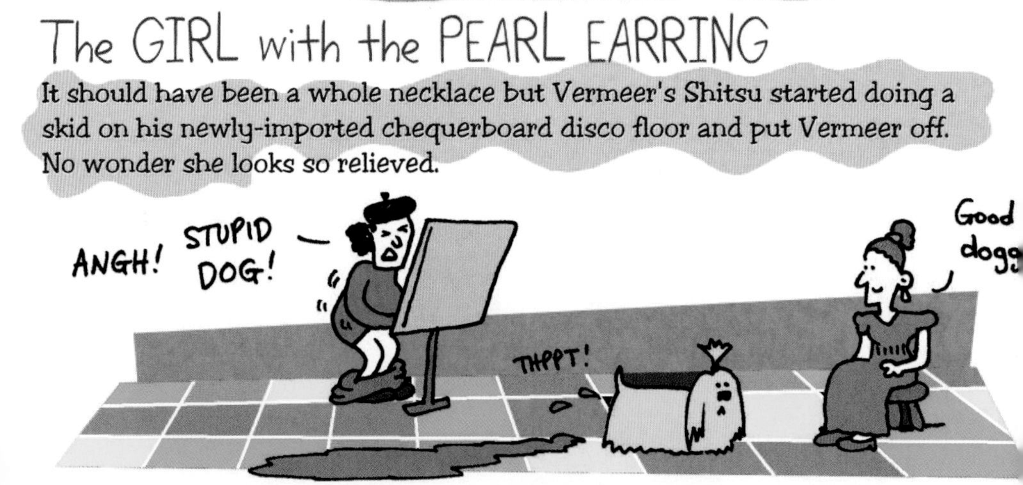
ANGH!
STUPID DOG!
THPPT!
Good dog

SUNFLOWERS

Few people know that this masterpiece is actually one of those moving images (plebeian art viewers all believe that art work should be viewed centrally). Stand to the left and the sunflowers are in full bloom, move to the right and the sunflowers wilt before your very eyes. A metaphor for the withering passion betwixt man and wife, the abhorrent disillusionment of monogamy, the death of sober sex. But, aha, move from right to left and it symbolises finding a new lover. Everyone loves a happy ending.

The CRYING WOMAN

The famous image is actually just a small fragment of the original painting, it was originally entitled 'Don't Get that Spunk in My Hair, Arsehole'. Pikasso's sobbing model used the majority of the canvas as a butt wipe in revenge for her sticky smelly hair - loo roll having not yet being invented. That came 3 years later in 1982.

Ha! Who's crying now?!

The MOANING LOSER

There's only one reason for the bored, indifferent expression on that frigid frump's face - she's waiting for de Vinci to ejaculate. Like all men (ie. a perv) he used a Polaroid to capture the moment, later simply colouring over it using crayons. If you scratch the painting in the Loovre you'll reveal the film underneath. Go on, dare you.

The WORLD IN ACTION Man

This is actually a self-portrait following de Vinci's lynching by the girl-group of the time, The (Pubic) Lice Girls, after they discovered he was doing them all, so they strapped him to an archery target. The producer of "World in Action" saw the piccie and wanted to buy it - provided de Vinci delete the arrows with correction fluid to remove the S&M overtones.

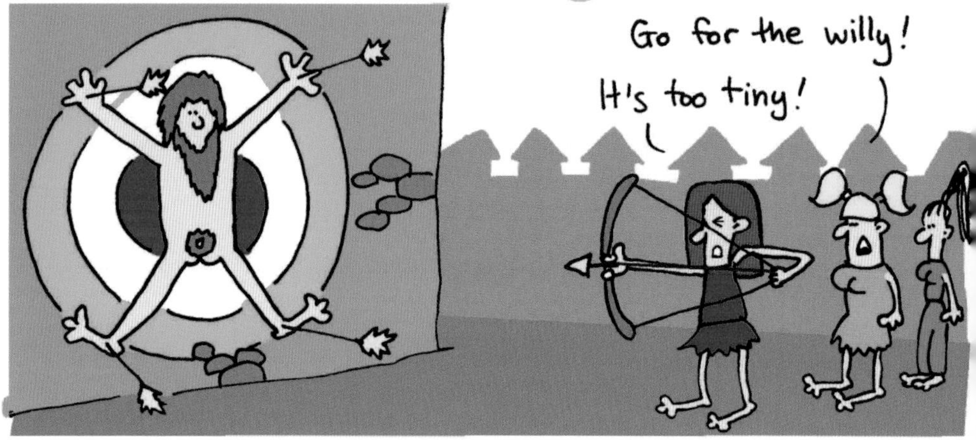

Go for the willy!
It's too tiny!

The HAYWAIN

A crudely-painted prototype for the much lauded "Where's Wally?" series. If you look hard enough you will actually see a peasant girl, Sarah Barrow, being rogered by her feudal landlord, Lord Walker.

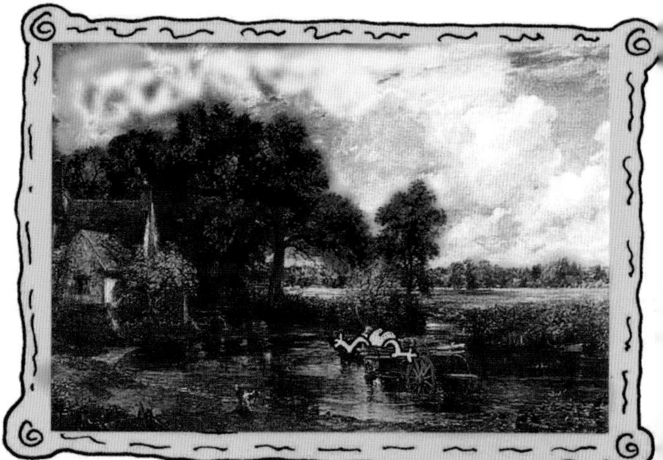

MAGIC EYE SERIES

Few people realise that Christopher Tyler's innocent-looking patterned picture craze of the late 80's actually contained XXX-rated imagery! This one shows fifteen naked models having sex in a vat of baby oil! Look closely for at least 7 hours and you'll see it!

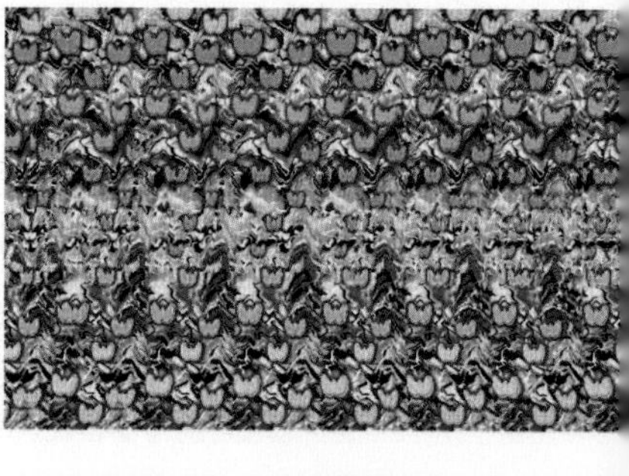

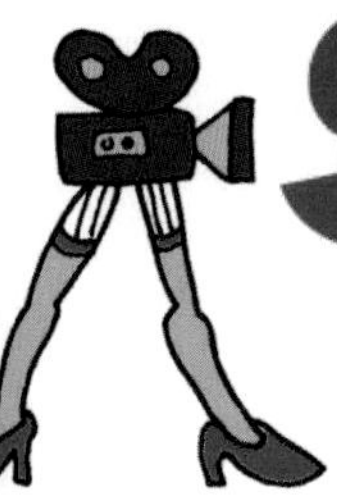

SEX in the MOVIES!

We're not talking X-rated dodgy porn or your "sexy" home movies. Or even the sex scenes in Hollywood films that you pretend not to enjoy watching when you're with your family. We're talking about all those nice family films where bored, puerile genius film editors have sneaked in subliminal images of pure filth for your subconscious eye to gawk at. Move over Jessica Rabbit, you slapper!

The Sound of Mooooooosic

Yep. There certainly was no-one quite like Maria... It seems the goat high on the hill wasn't quite so lonely after all. The Hills were alive with the sound of bonking!

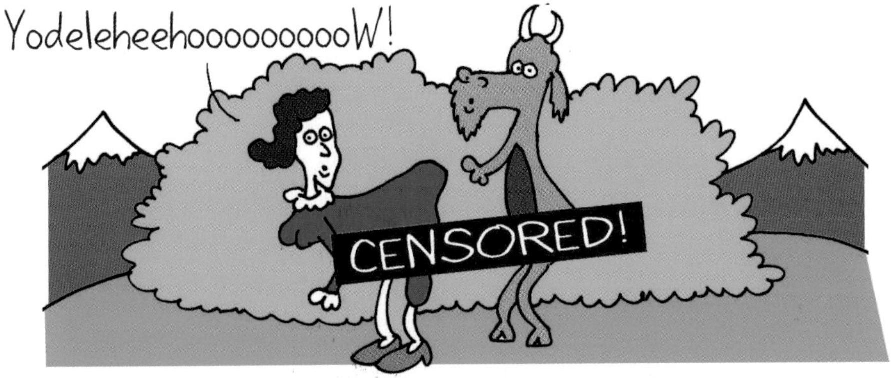
YodeleheehoooooooooW!
CENSORED!

he Wizard of Ass

ever mind the heart, brain and courage. The only thing the Tinman, Scarecrow and Lion ere missing were morals. That's why Dorothy just wanted to go home. Prissy cow.

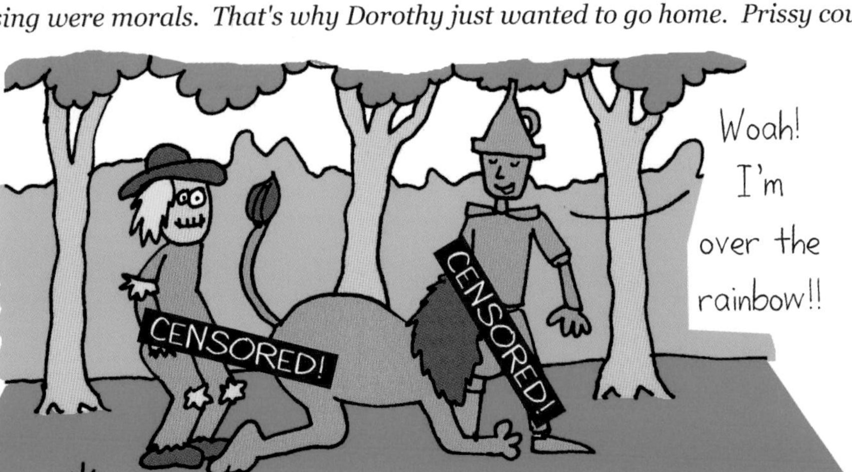
Woah! I'm over the rainbow!!
CENSORED!
CENSORED!

Mary Popped In For a Quickie

This hidden image reveals the real reason why nannies are hired: not to look after the children at all, but the HUSBAND! She let him 'poppin' whenever he liked! It seems a spoonful of sugar helps the husband go down!

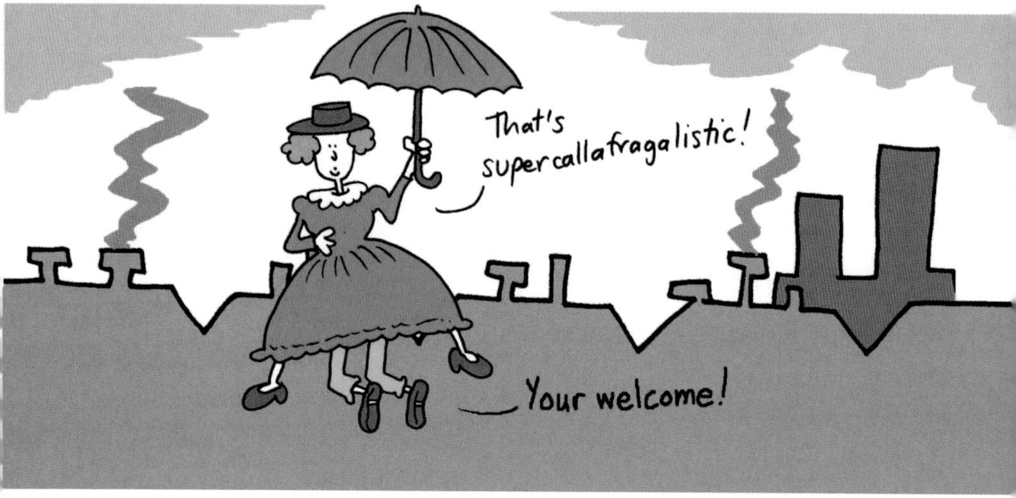
That's supercallafragalistic!
Your welcome!

Finding Homo

This secret scene is a poignant, revealing comment of our times. Like all fathers Homo's dad was GLAD his son had vanished, leaving him free to look for a new wife to replace the one who'd snuffed it! In fact, Homo's Dad found love with the whale, Moby Big Dick. That blow hole's not for breathing, you know. And do you want to know what they did with their oscar? Clue: it's not gold any more!

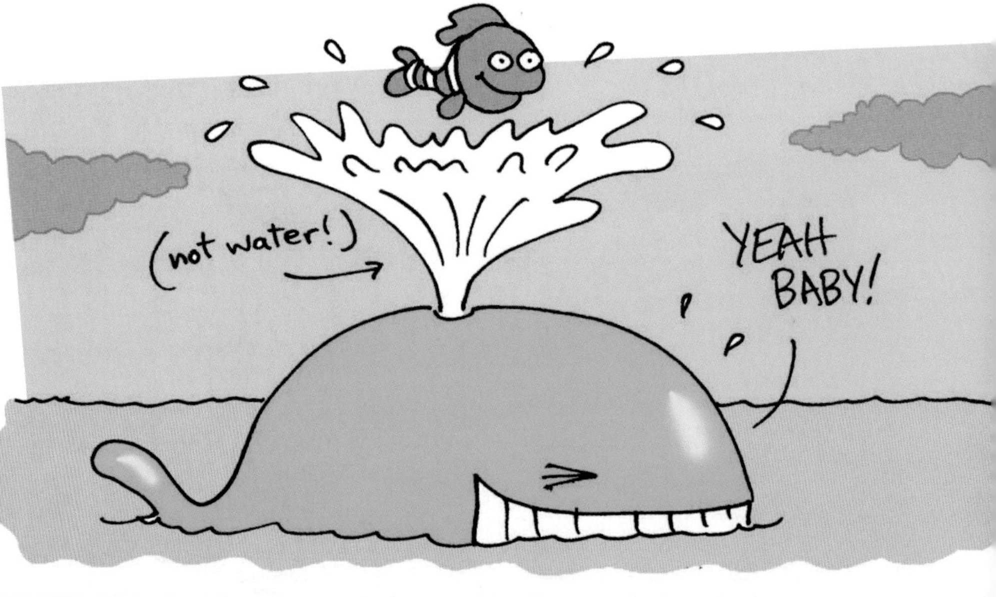
(not water!)
YEAH BABY!

›sycho

atboy Hitch edited in this image after secretly filming Janet Lea on set showering in ɛr trailer. He was not only disgusted at discovering a woman actually pleasured ɛrself, but that they could do it in such a shocking way - shower heads are for LEANING!! AND she forgot › hang it back afterwards! ut Janet Lea had the last laugh :he knew he'd been filming) nd broke the shower curtain ı the famous scene because ıe knew Hitchy wasn't ısured for damages. Ha!

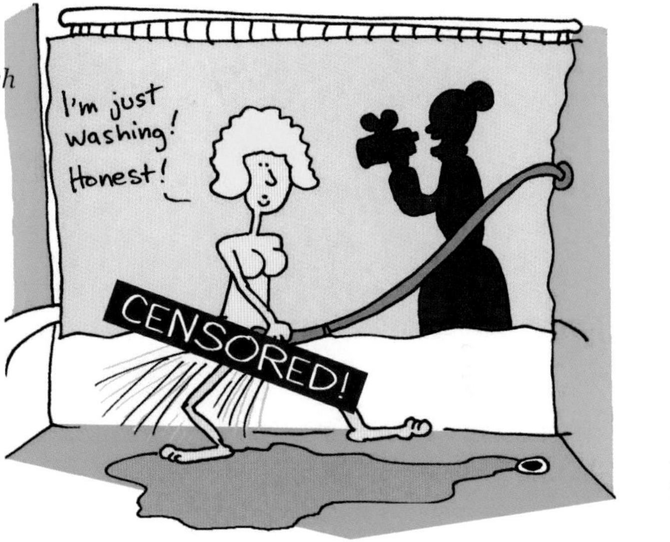
I'm just washing! Honest!
CENSORED!

›ulp Friction

You'll never want a "Royale with Cheese" again (hmmm, or maybe you will). Following the discovery of these subliminal images, a certain fast food chain were forced to create an advertising campaign based purely on hygiene (as if its customers care about hygiene!).

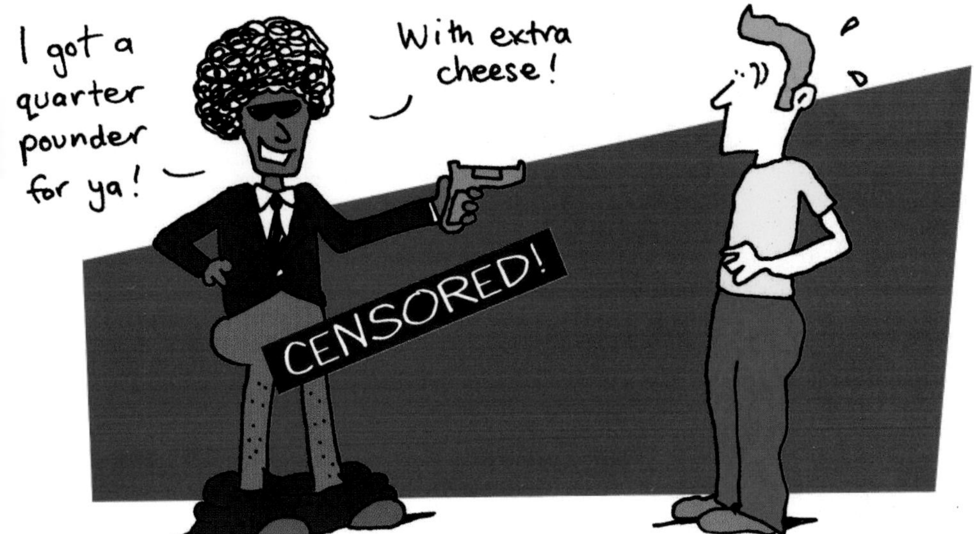
I got a quarter pounder for ya!
With extra cheese!
CENSORED!

HOW TO *Lose your Virginity*

STAGE ONE - Clear the Area!

In order to lose your virginity correctly, you must wait for your parents to go out, as it not only adds to the excitement, but is slightly more comfortable than your school locker. Ideally, they should be further away than the back garden because your ageing parents now suffer from incontinence and will make frequent trips back inside to empty their colostomy bags. Warning - colostomy bags make deadly weapons!!

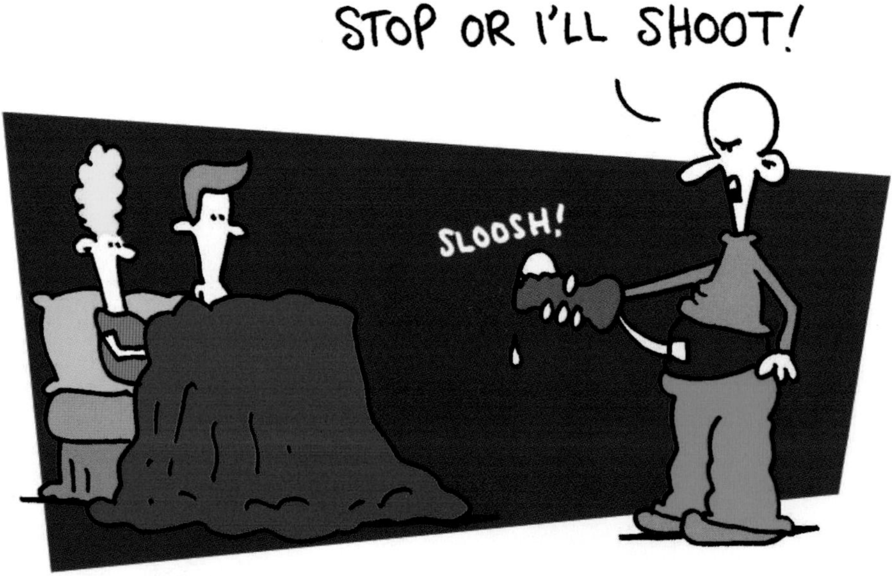
STOP OR I'LL SHOOT!
SLOOSH!

STAGE TWO - Location!

Now, which room to do it in? The kitchen? Too many sharp implements. The Living Room? Too many family photos. The Bathroom? Too many pubes on the floor. Your bedroom? Too much like being unfaithful to your hand. That only leaves your parents' double bed. Perfect! Just be aware you may discover marital aids that your parents have hidden!

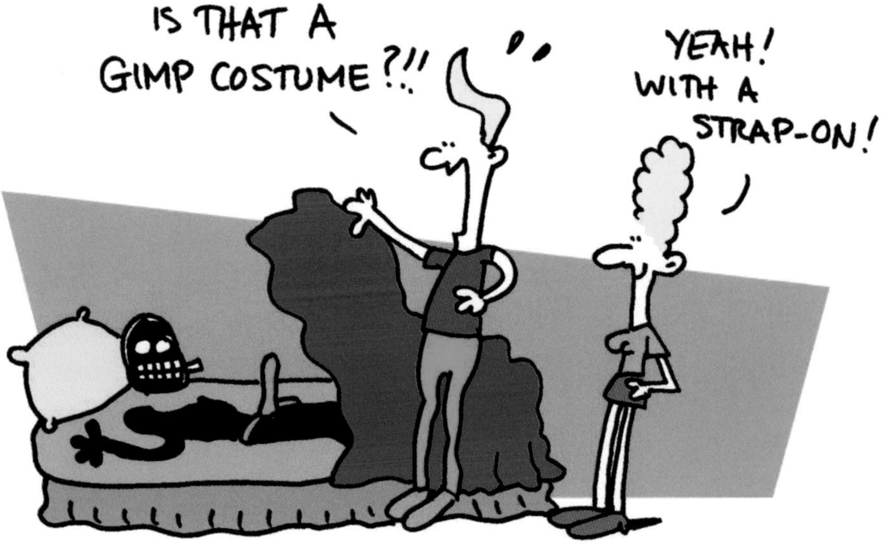
IS THAT A GIMP COSTUME ?!!
YEAH! WITH A STRAP-ON!

STAGE THREE - Prepare the Boudoir!

1. Barricade the door with heavy objects to prevent 'curious sibling' invasion!

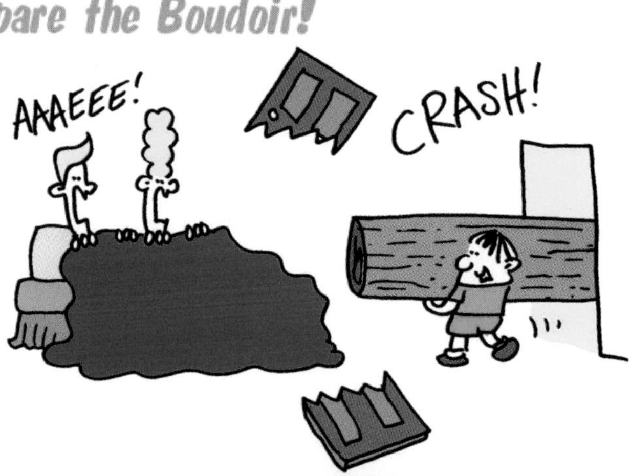
AAAEEE!
CRASH!

B) Romantically drape 2&4 old sheets and towels over the sex-slab. For the ensuing mess, have bleach, bucket and rubber gloves handy (in case of excessive wall splatter).

Ready

C) Light scented candles. Not for the romance factor but to disguise the noxious stench of nervous fartings.

≈ TOOT! ≈

FWOOM!

OOPS!

STAGE FOUR - Foreplay!

Now, stand facing each other and play the "Who can Get their Kit Off the Fastest" game. It's important not to laugh at the other person's bits at this point. Then simply fiddle with anything that is pink and hard as if you were tuning a radio.

Oh dear. Poor reception.

TWIDDLE!

STAGE FIVE - The Dirty Act!

Right, now you're ready to stare lovingly-ish into each other's genitals. Try your bestest not to grimace and whisper sweet algebra into each other's waxy ears.

COR!
UGH!

Yes, you're finally ready. . . for a pillow fight! Show no mercy. The winner takes all... your sweeties. Continue the fun with a sweaty session of mutual trampolining. See who can bounce the highest! Wee-hee.

CRASH!
YOU DIDN'T CLEAN YOUR BUM PROPERLY.

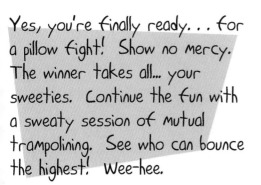

Now, you're REALLY ready. Writhe about comically like you've seen in the movies. Finally, spasm away like you've just been shot by a 44 magnum and struck by a hit and run spaceship.

AAAAHHH! OOOH! OOOOH!
I HAVEN'T STARTED YET.

Next, wait for the front door to open before the famous mad scrabble back to the living room. Indeed, why not add to the excitement by having a bash at making the parental bed! Remember not to leave any tell-tale cuddly toys behind!

WHO'S JONNY IS THIS ?!
NOT MINE. TOO BIG.

SLAP-FREE CHAT-UP LINES!

Astoundingly, your mediocre looks, permanent whiff of cabbage and accidental spitting whilst speaking, isn't always enough to spontaneously seduce your victim on sight. If money doesn't do the trick either, resort to these foolproof lines.

MY FATHER OWNS A BREWERY!
I OWN STRIPPER TASSELS!
I NEVER WANT CHILDREN!
I'LL NEVER LEAVE MY POOEY G-STRINGS ON THE FLOOR!
I EARN IN EXCESS OF £40K PER ANNUM.
I LOVE FOOTBALL!
I HATE CLOTHES SHOPPING!
I'M A LESBIAN!
I LOVE VATCHING PORN!
I LOVE GIVING BLOW JOBS!

How to Flirt! (successfully)

MANY PEOPLE WRONGLY BELIEVE THAT FLIRTING IS THE KEY TO SUCCESSFUL SCORING BALLDERDASH! THE ACTUAL SECRET OF SEDUCTION IS PLAYING THE SPOONS, BUT THIS REQUIRES REAL GENIUS SO THE REST OF YOU WILL HAVE TO OPT FOR FRIGID TRADITIONAL TECHNIQUES

Eyes

TRY TO MAINTAIN EYE CONTACT AT ALL TIMES!

You have beautiful ... eyes.

Hey!

APPLY SPIDERY FAKE EYELASHES AND BAT THEM AT HIM ALLURINGLY!

WAFT

AAAAAAA

Mouth

LICK LIPS SLOWLY AND PROVOCATIVELY, THEN SHOW HIM HOW BIG YOUR MOUTH CAN STRETCH!

Not wide enough baby!

Mirroring

PRETEND YOU'RE KINDRED SPIRITS BY COPYING THEIR EVERY MOVE!

GET OUT!

Giggling

LAUGH AT ANYTHING AND EVERYTHING THEY SAY! NO MATTER WHAT!

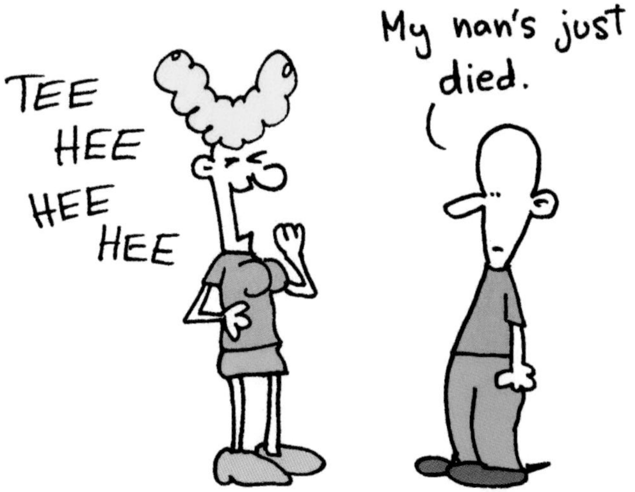
TEE HEE HEE HEE
My nan's just died.

Touching

PATTING THEM LIGHTLY ON THE ARM IS TOO SUBTLE. GO STRAIGHT FOR WOBBLY BITS!

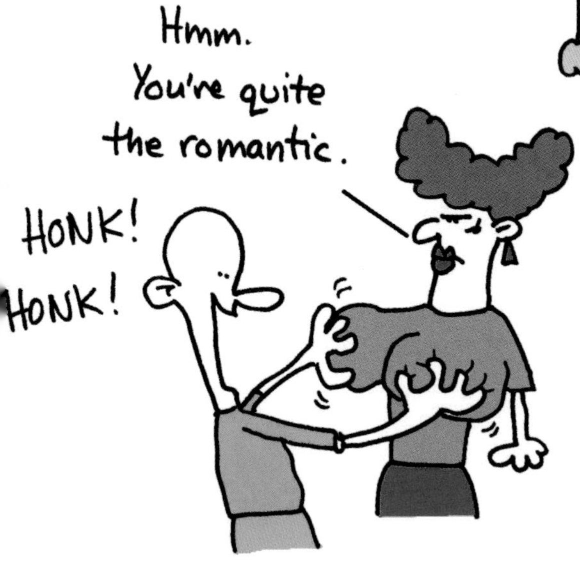
Hmm. You're quite the romantic.
HONK! HONK!

Talking

NO MATTER HOW UGLY YOU ARE, INVADE THEIR PERSONAL SPACE AND TALK SOFTLY IN THEIR EAR – THEY WILL EXPERIENCE THE FAMOUS 'BUM SHIVER' SYNDROME! WORKS EVERY TIME!

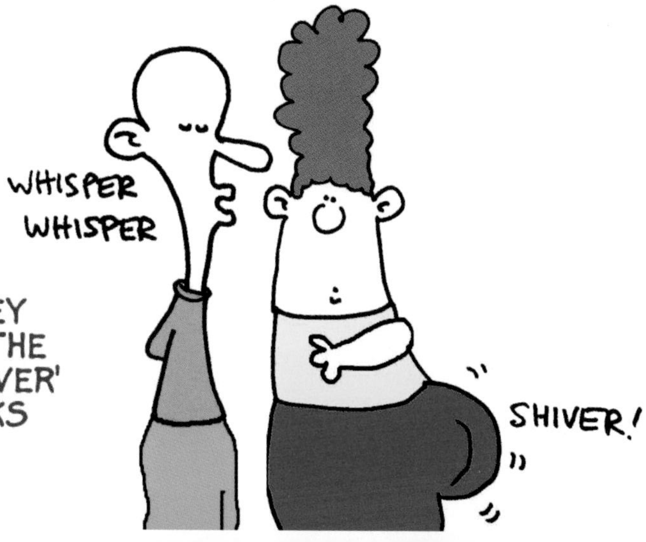
WHISPER WHISPER
SHIVER!

FOREPLAY TIPS!

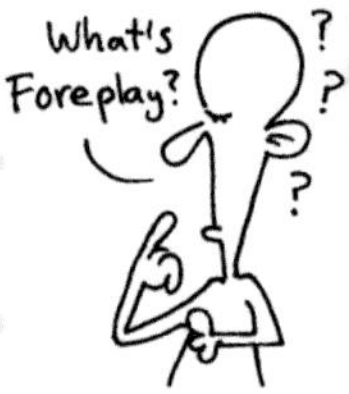
What's Foreplay?
? ? ?

Not only is foreplay very dangerous, it's also extremely tedious. Especially with someone you know. In fact, having to bother with foreplay puts 97% of couples off having sex at all. So, to stop the human race dying out in 2043, here are a few tips for making foreplay bearable...

1. VISUAL AIDS!

BLINDFOLD!

Pull the old 'blindfolds are erotic' scam on your partner to hide their oh-so familiar, hideous features from your precious eyes.

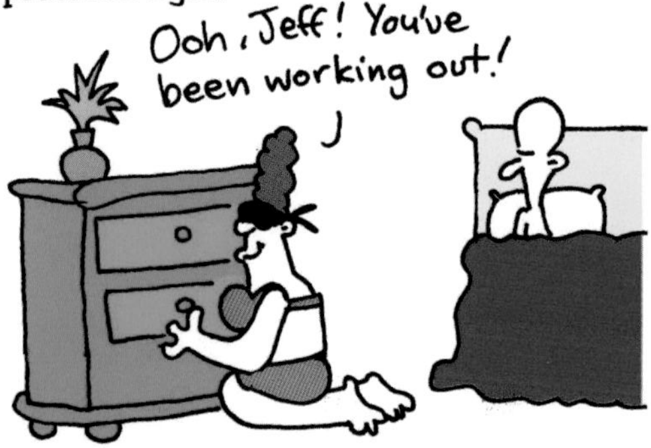
Ooh, Jeff! You've been working out!

MASKS!

Whilst at work, spend all your time photocopying your fave celebrity's face to make an attractive sex mask! (Never choose Richard or Judy!)

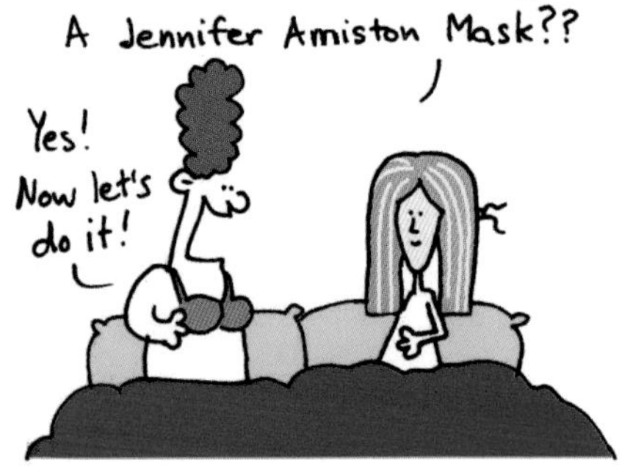
A Jennifer Amiston Mask??
Yes! Now let's do it!

SEASIDE BOARDS!

Increase your partner's attractiveness without expensive gym memberships or reconstructive surgery. Simply steal a muscle man/big busted lady board for an immediate makeover!

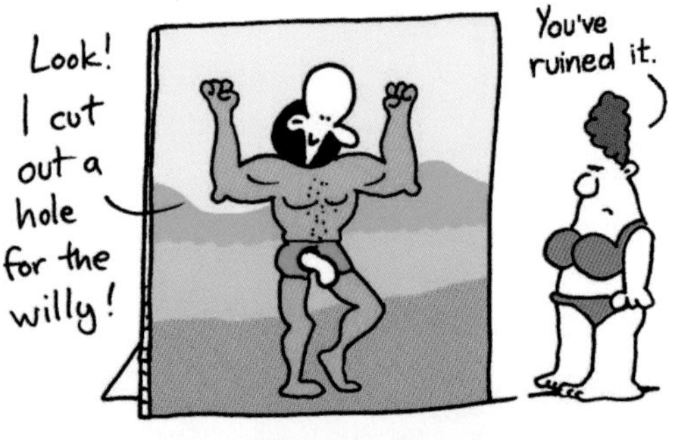
Look! I cut out a hole for the willy!
You've ruined it.

TATTOOS!

Drag your partner down to the nearest parlour and have the perfect physique tattooed on their body. Try to ignore the rolls of flab hanging out at the sides.

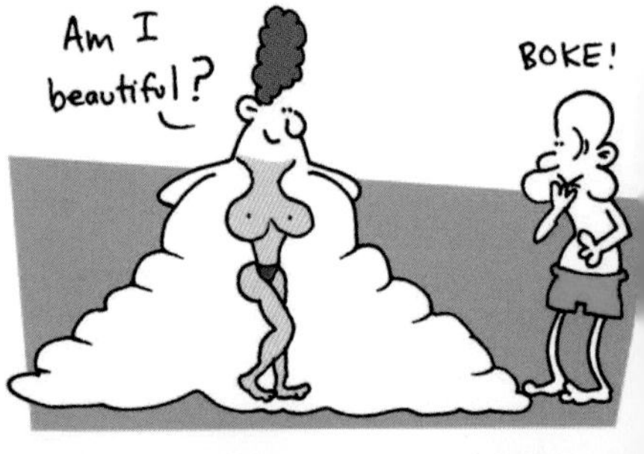
Am I beautiful?
BOKE!

2. TALKING DIRTY!

Under no circumstances should talking dirty be attempted by anyone with a posh accent. It just sounds ridiculous. Neither should the Welsh - too much phlegm. Neither should the Scottish - it just sounds threatening. And neither should the Irish - it just sounds like you're telling a joke. Come to mention it, if you come from, er ANYWHERE, neither should you. It just sounds naff. But if you must make some kind of encouraging sound, use this guide to tolerable sex noises . . .

"MMMMmmmmmm!"

Use this when your partner does something remotely interesting. Don't adopt a monotone as it'll sound like there's a mozzy in the room, and remember to trail off at the end to avoid sounding like a nutter.

"Ooooo...aaaaaaahh!"

For females only. Use upon his light-sabre entry to show your pleasure, with more 'aaaaaaah' if he's paranoid about being crap in bed.

"Ngh! Ngh! Ngh Ngh!"

Use near end of pumping session to indicate pending real/fake orgasm. If bored or you're about to miss your favourite TV show, speed up grunts in hope of conning other person to come more quickly.

"Yes! Yes! Yes Yes!"

A braggard exclamation used by those living in shared accomodation (students, nurses, convicts) to show off to all and sundry that you're having sex and they're not. Make sure you shout your OWN name to make sure everyone knows it's you getting the action.

"AAAARRGGGGHHHH!"

For females only. VITAL if he's paranoid about his size! This'll make him think he's got the longest plunger you've ever cleaned your drain with.

"Zzzzzzzzzzzzzzzz..."

Marvellously rich, sub-textual affirmation of a joint dismal performance when you've both gone through the machinations of intercourse merely to kid yourselves that you still have a sex life.

3. APHRODISIACS!

If music be the food of love, then traditional aphrodisiacs are the Andrew Lloyd Webbers of the gourmet world.

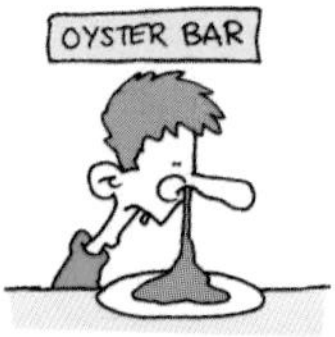
OYSTER BAR

FACT: All oysters purchased from shops or restaurants are in actual fact the by-product of gangly teenage boys' bogey excesses.

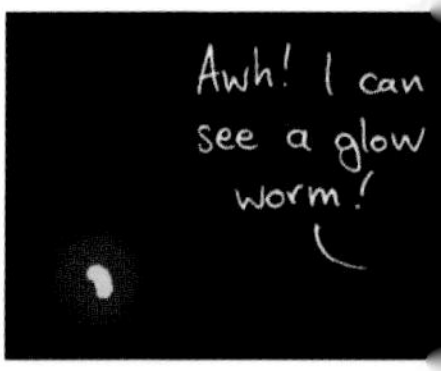
Awh! I can see a glow worm!

FACT: Asparagus spears not only make your pee-pee smell rancid, they also cause the male member to glow in the dark (which may not be a good thing).

So, it's time to try some REAL aphrodisiacs that ACTUALLY WORK....

THE BEER GOGGLEDISIAC!

Ingredients:
1-2+ desperate individuals
1 bucket (for initial mixing, then for puke collection later)
1 line of pumps and optics
(try a pub, supermarket, or naff neighbour)
1 camera (for blackmailing purposes later)
1 day off work

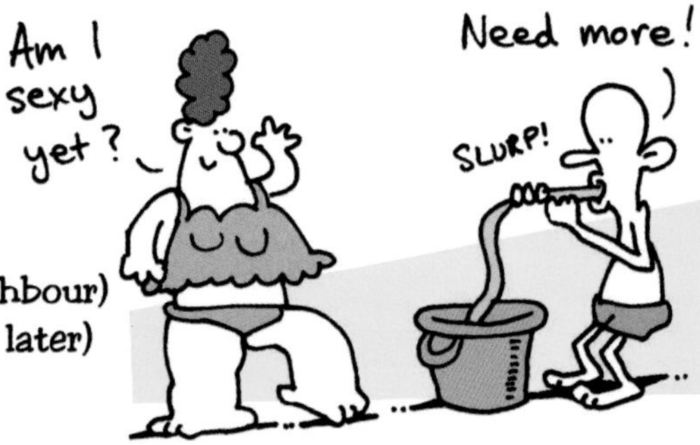
Am I sexy yet?
Need more!
SLURP!

Method: Mix the optics and beer with the individuals as quickly as possible. When a pukey consistency has been achieved, the individuals will be ready, willing and vaguely able to engage in sexy business.

THE CHIPDISIAC!

It's well-known that females are more turned on by chips than anything else (even shopping) - especially if stolen from partner using distraction tactics like saying "What's that over there?" Therefore, to get in her chastity pants, buy some chips and let her steal them all. It's more effective in getting her in the sack than going down on bended knee.

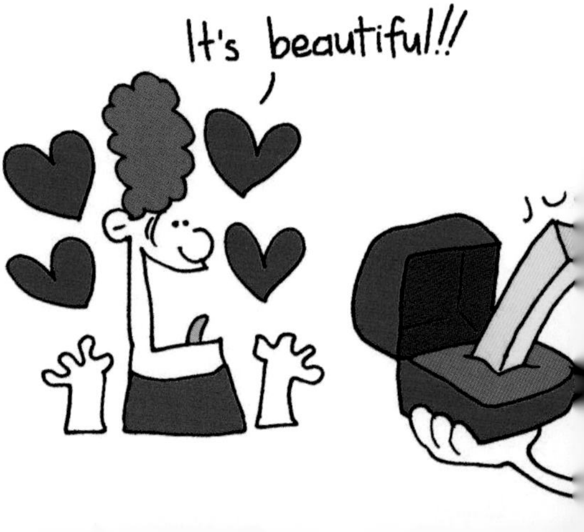
It's beautiful!!

THE CHOCOLATE SACRIFICEDISIAC!

Men, resort to this if she's been particularly frigid. Buy her a big (cheap) box of chocs and commit the ultimate act of self-sacrifice to lure her into your hairy lair... by eating all the minging GINGER chocolates. AAAAAAAAAARGHHHHH!!!!! Then again, what's wrong with celibacy?

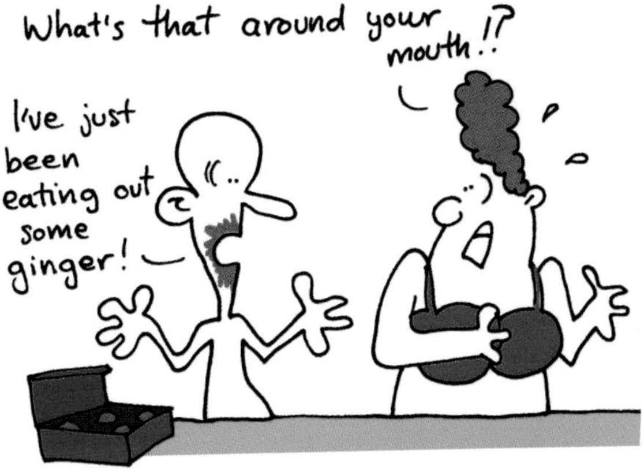
What's that around your mouth!?
I've just been eating out some ginger!

THE VACUUMDISIAC!

If a male applies this domestic appliance to the female she'll succumb to all requests. Yes, even THAT one.

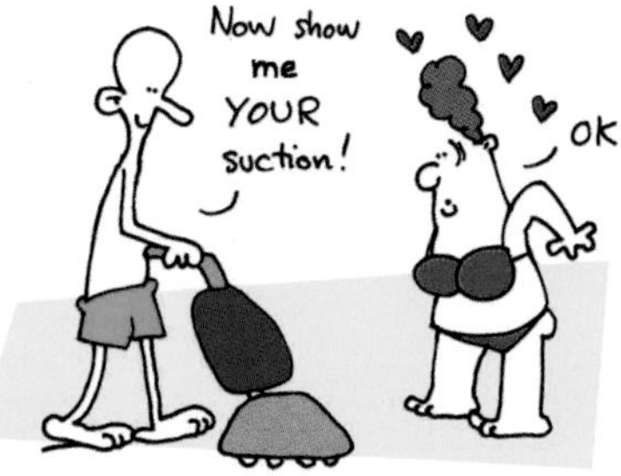
Now show me YOUR suction!
OK!

4. FANTASY ROLE PLAY!

There comes a point in every relationship when copious amounts of alcohol, 2 minutes of late night free TV porn, and hollow promises of DIY jobs just don't cut it any more. You now have no choice but to try fantasy role play - that's if you can stop sniggering.

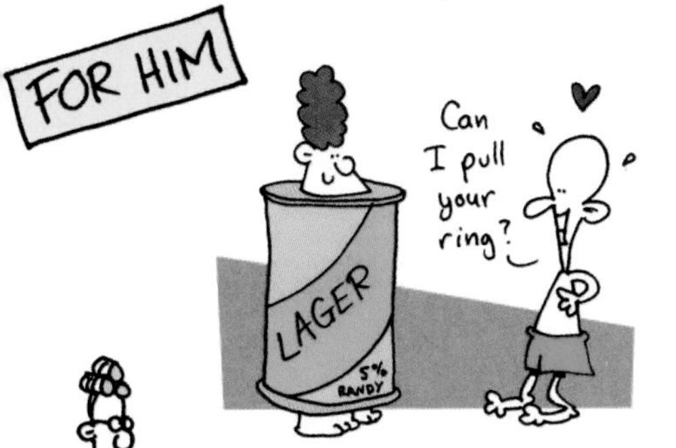
FOR HIM
Can I pull your ring?
LAGER
5% RANDY

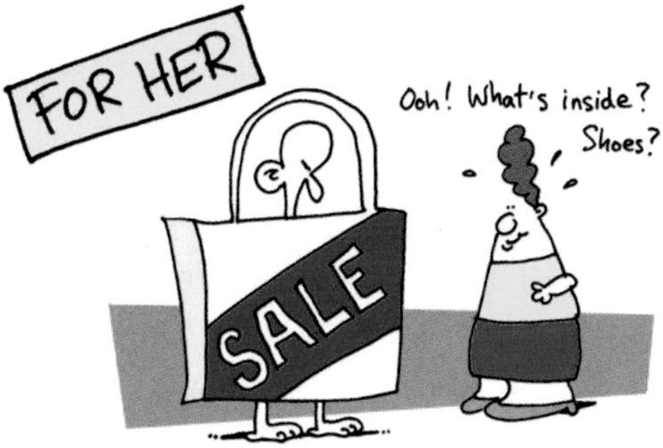
FOR HER
Ooh! What's inside? Shoes?
SALE

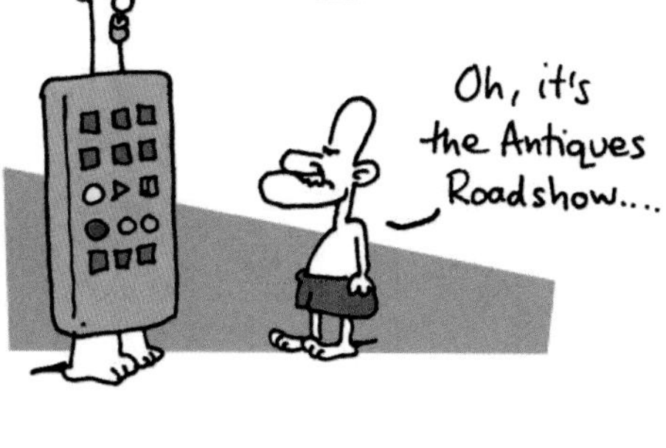
Oh, it's the Antiques Roadshow....

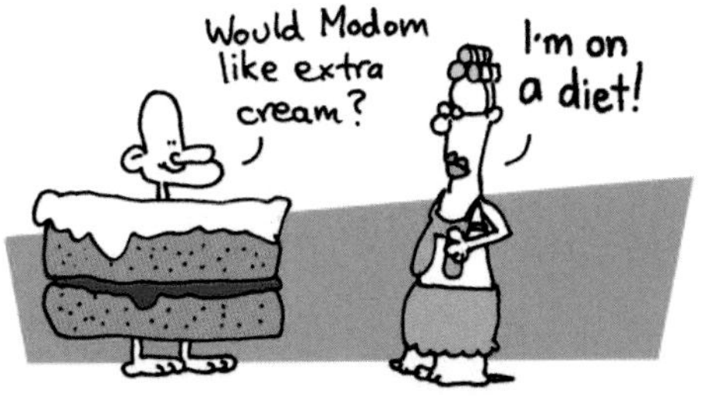
Would Modom like extra cream?
I'm on a diet!

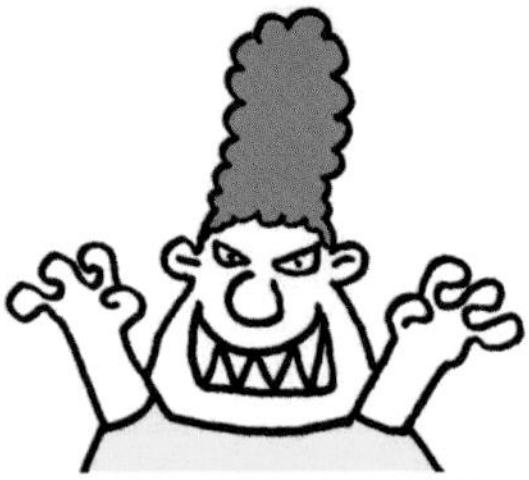

A BLOKE'S GUIDE TO ALTERNATIVE CONTRACEPTION

Men, wake up and smell the nappy! Women use sex to trap men into fatherhood! Think about it. Who takes responsibility for contraception in a relationship? Not the man, that's for sure. And the last bastion of penis power, condoms, are easily tampered with (long nails!!). Remember, if a woman ***ever*** initiates sex it's ***only*** cos she's trying to trap you into lifelong parenthood! The **only** foolproof way to avoid being tricked into this hell **is to not have sex** with the evil schemer in the first place*. So, follow this irresponsible guide to not getting up the duff.

THE CAP

Wear a naff hat (tip: 'borrow' one from a senile passer-by), adopt a silly high voice (helpful suggestion: squeeze your balls), and acquire some buck-teeth (perhaps mug a rabbit or a royal family member).

Result? She won't want sex with you for months! There's an added bonus too, you can earn a handsome second income playing the working men's clubs (12p per hour/14p in House of Lords).

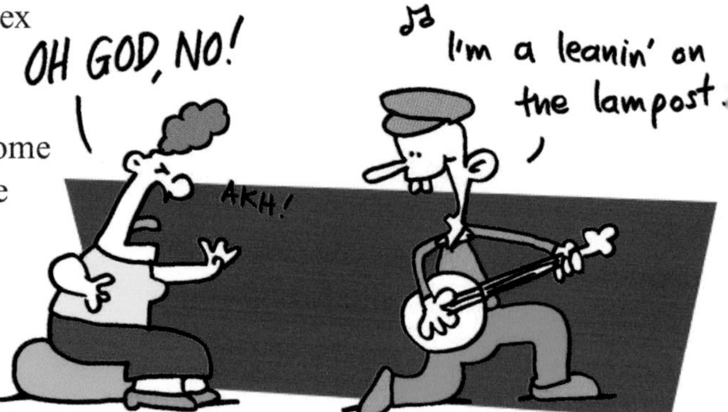
OH GOD, NO!
AKH!
I'm a leanin' on the lampost.

THE DIAPHRAM

This method can be quite fiddly – what with inserting pints on belly, and sticking out your diaphragm *so* much that it would impress an Ethiopian. But well worth the trouble as her repulsion can last for weeks.

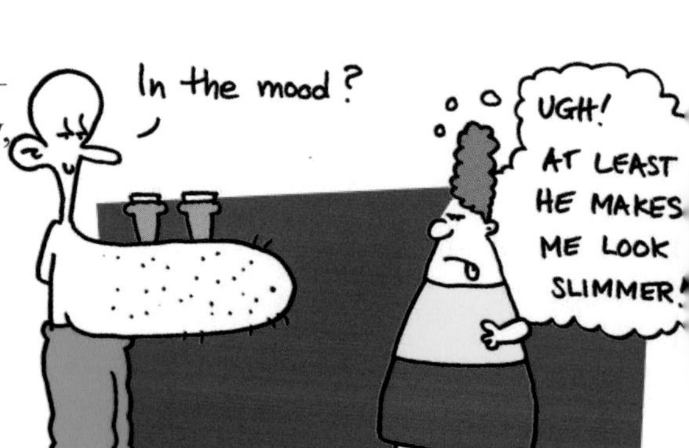
In the mood?
UGH!
AT LEAST HE MAKES ME LOOK SLIMMER!

*This becomes easier over time as she lets herself go, and turns into your mother-in-law.

ORAL CONTRACEPTION

'he first male oral contraceptive is a uaranteed immediate turn-off - take ebab with chilli sauce! It's painless to wallow, easy to remember - once a ay, and also acts as an inexpensive olonic. Wooooosh.

Give us a kiss!

THE WITHDRAWAL METHOD

Nothing is a more effective contraception than the woman thinking you're a tight-wad or broke. Now you're free to join your mates for a drink or strip club (tip: remember the old 'money on elastic' ruse).

BALANCE
£4329
Oh dear! I'm skint!
Bye then!

STERILISATION

A last resort. There's no going back once you begin this method of contraception. Start sterilising and cleaning - she'll be so gutted and bitter that you're better at cleaning than her, she'll never want sex again (tip: if you opt for this method it will also reveal that you're gay).

Tum te tum!
AAAAA!!

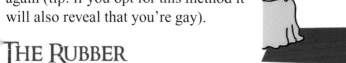

THE RUBBER

If there's a footie match on that she's determined to stop you watching by offering herself, then fight back by simply slipping on a full body deep sea diving suit. However, be warned, some women will actually think this means you're into 'muff diving'.

Get me a beer, luv.
HMPH!

THE COIL

This is a cheap, readily available method of contraception ideal for when she's too insistent, had too many alcopops and wants to make a home porn movie (it'll only end in tears. Hers). Just lay a chocolate cobra in your throne. Plus, there's the added pleasure of simultaneously being able to fragrance your whole home.

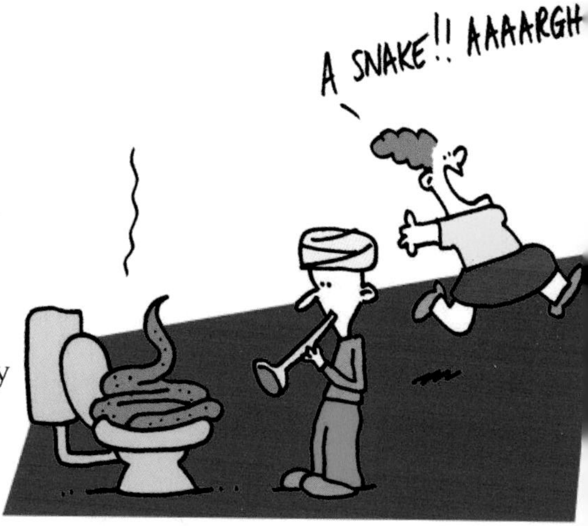

A SNAKE!! AAAARGH

THE SPONGE

'Tis an historical truth that women never ever pay for anything, or even pretend to offer, preferring instead to sponge off their sucker partners. Revenge is yours with this instant method of contraception – with a thousand examples of her sponging at your disposal, she'll storm off in a huff (to raid your pockets for change).

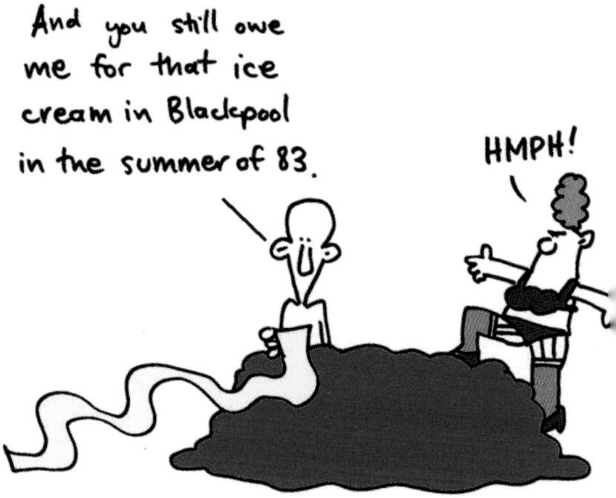

And you still owe me for that ice cream in Blackpool in the summer of 83.
HMPH!

THE NATURAL METHOD

Simply go a few days without trimming those excess nose, eyebrow, and ear hairs! She'll balk at your wolfman appearance and refuse to come anywhere near you! Act hurt, then insist that copulation can go no further because she doesn't love you in your natural state. Ignore her threat that she'll stop doing her bikini line. She's bluffing.

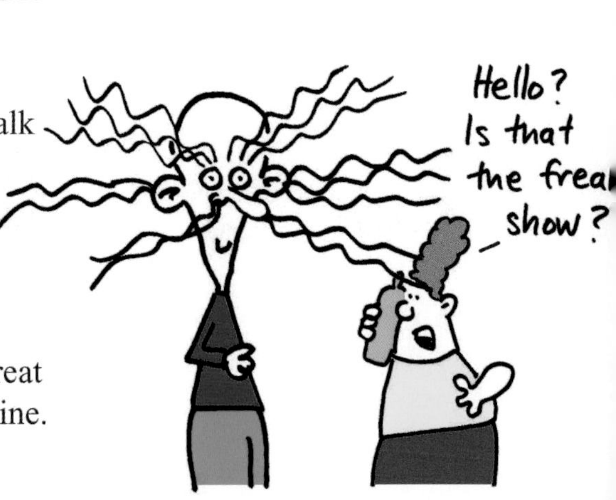

Hello? Is that the frea show?

The JOY OF SEX

The REAL positions!

Spend Hours on Foreplay to Turn Her On

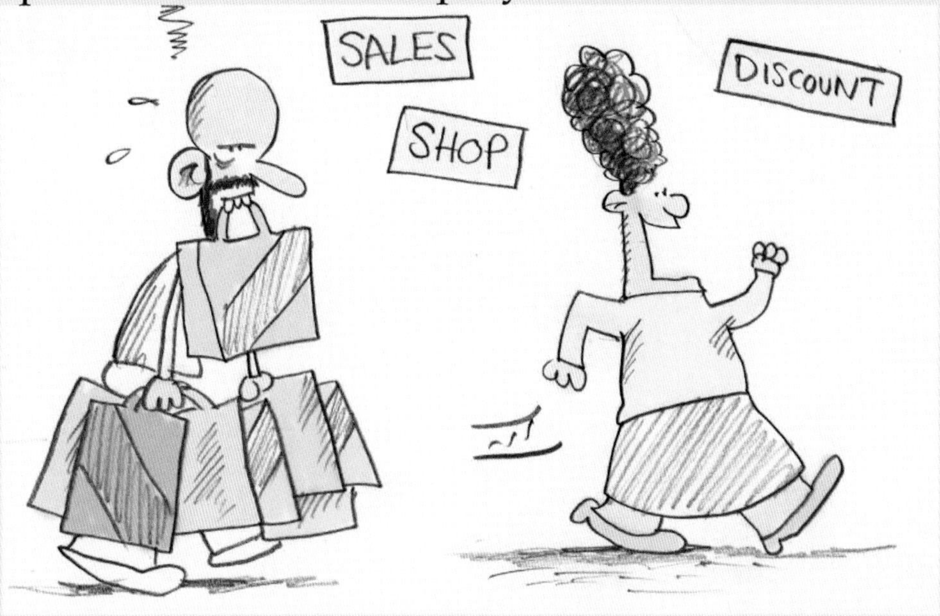
SALES
DISCOUNT
SHOP

Satisfy Her Needs in Bed

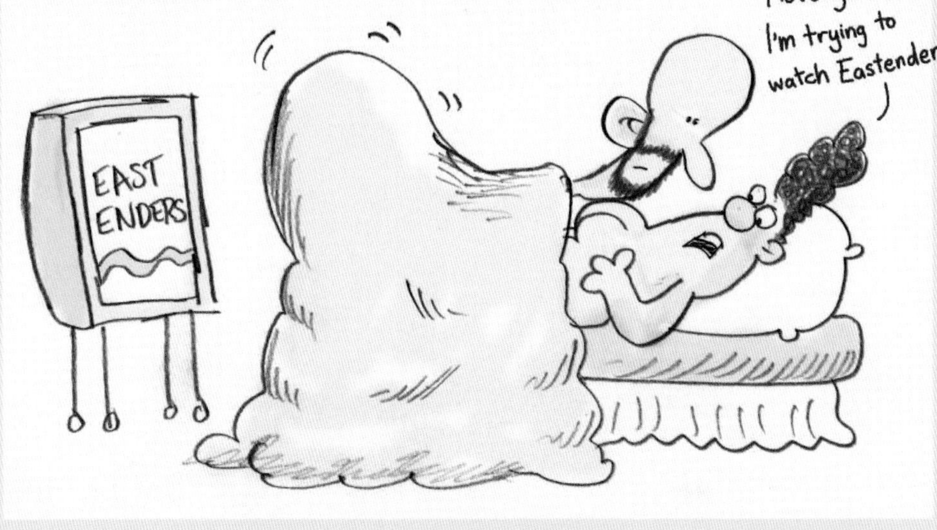
Move your bum I'm trying to watch Eastenders!
EAST ENDERS

Never Eat Curry the Night Before

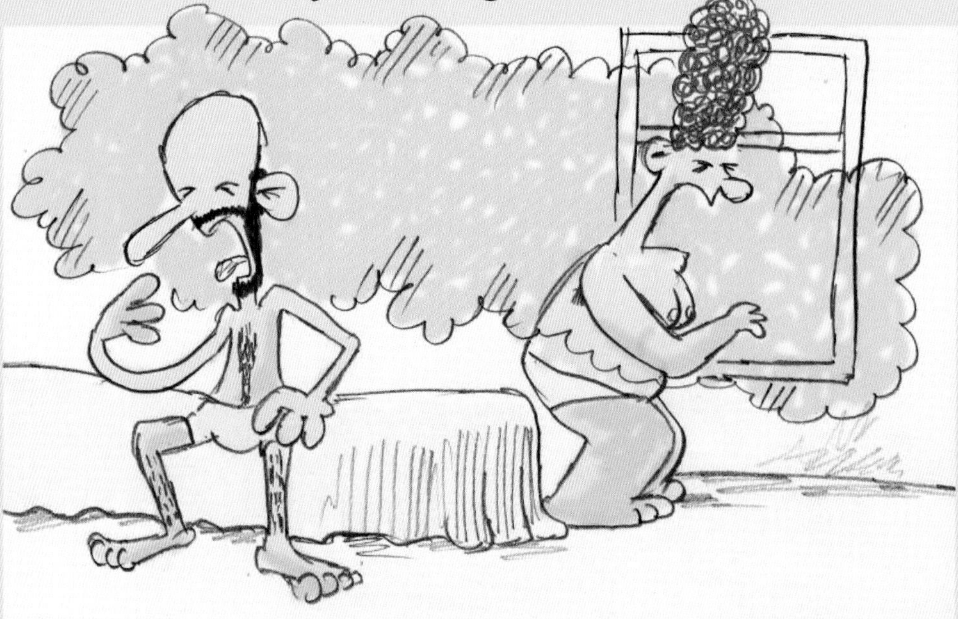

Spend Time on Oral Sex

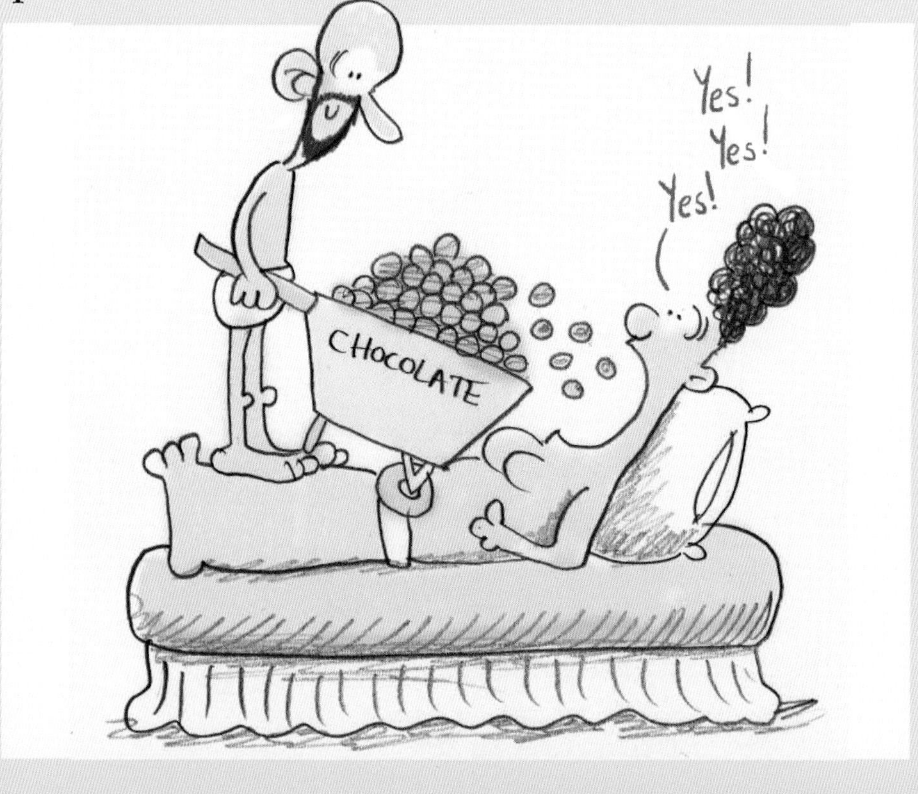
Yes!
Yes!
Yes!
CHOCOLATE

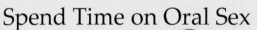

Pleasure Him by Tickling his Anal Gland

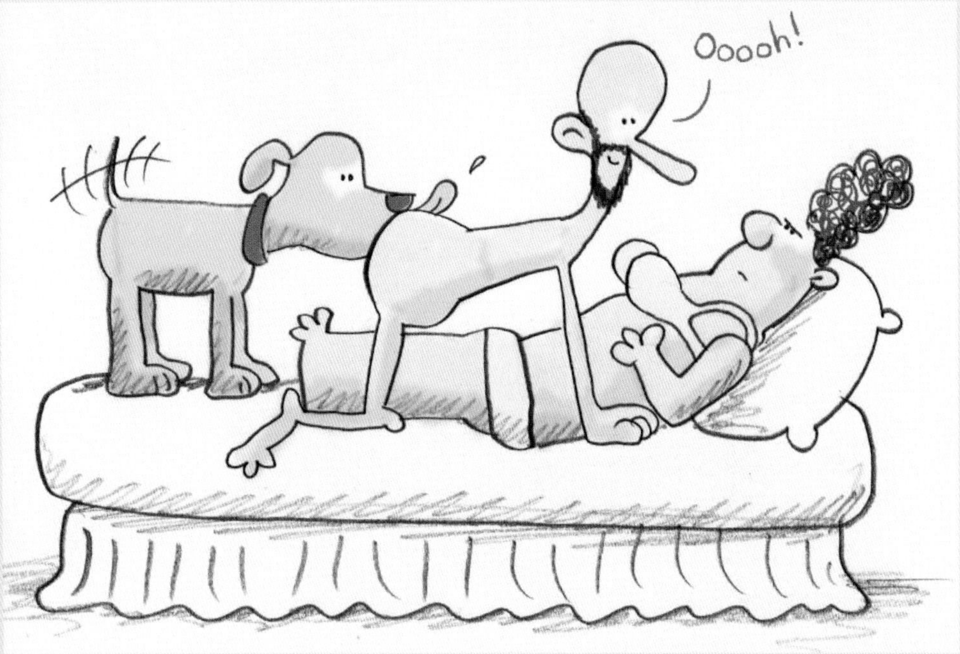
Ooooh!

Enjoy a Romantic Bath Together

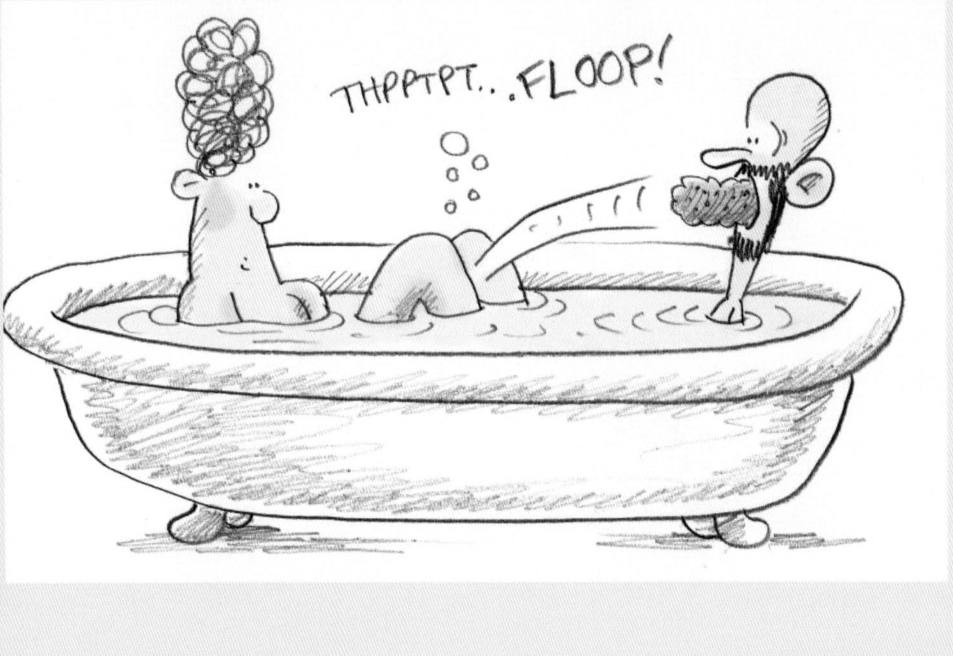
THPPTPT...FLOOP!

Experiment with the 'Spoons' Position

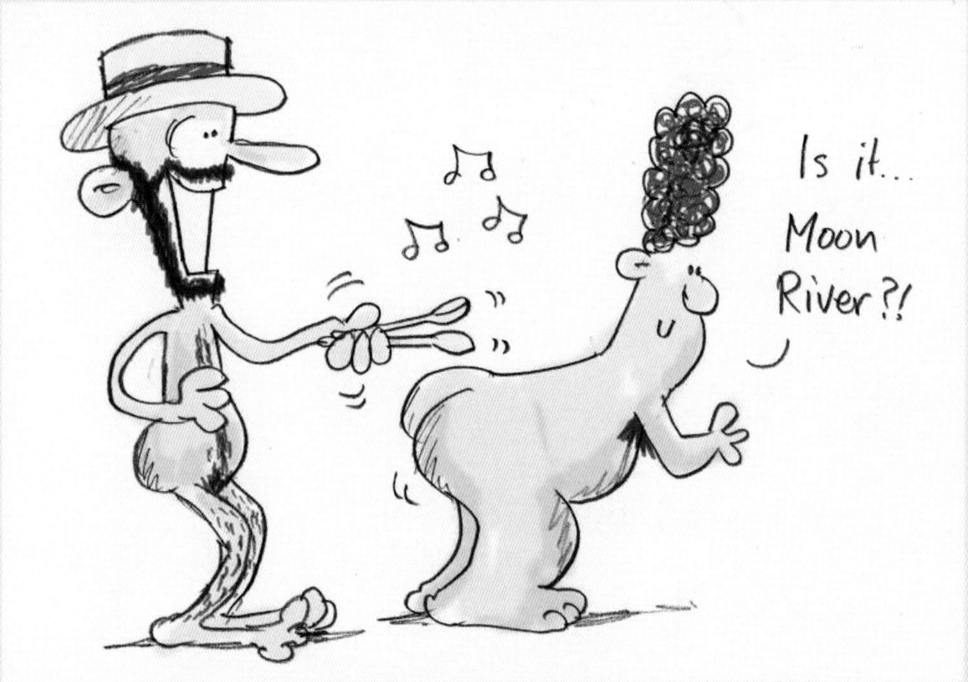
Is it...
Moon
River?!

Cover your Partner in Chocolate Sauce

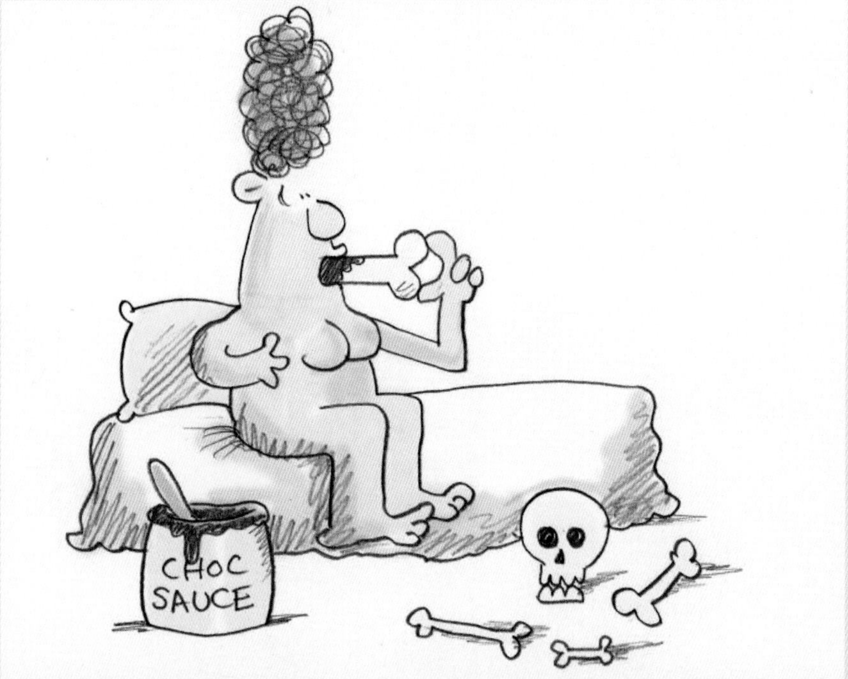
CHOC
SAUCE

Try the '69' Position

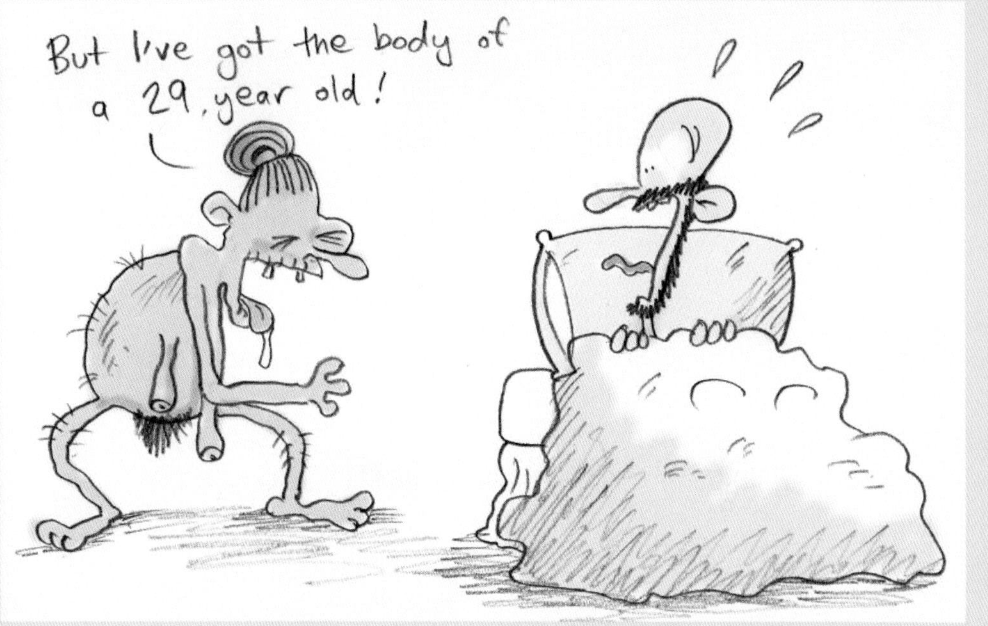
But I've got the body of a 29 year old!

Never Blow Off During Anal Sex

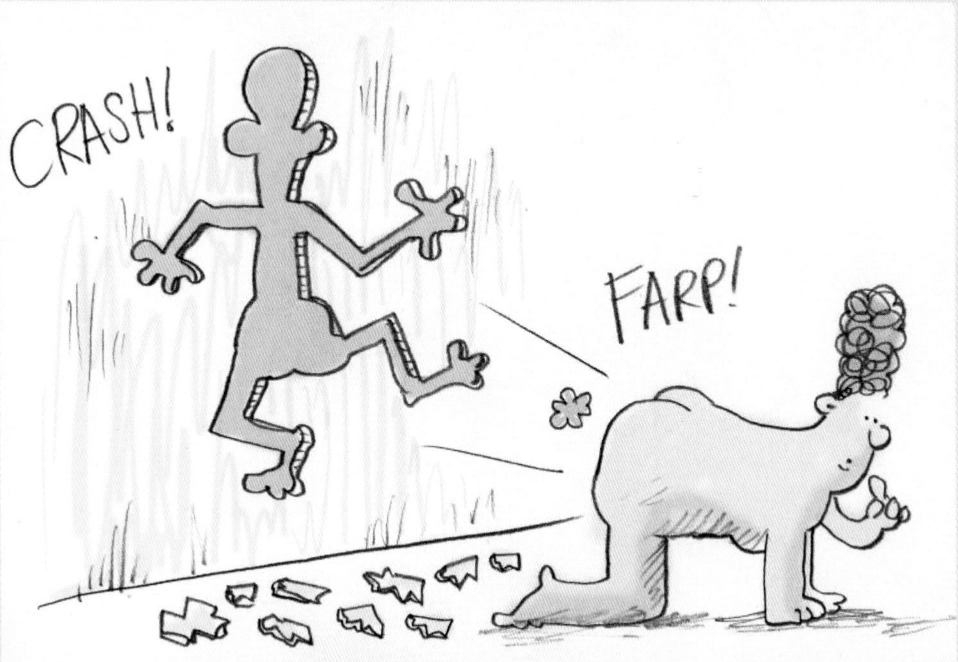
CRASH!
FARP!

SEX AROUND the WORLD!

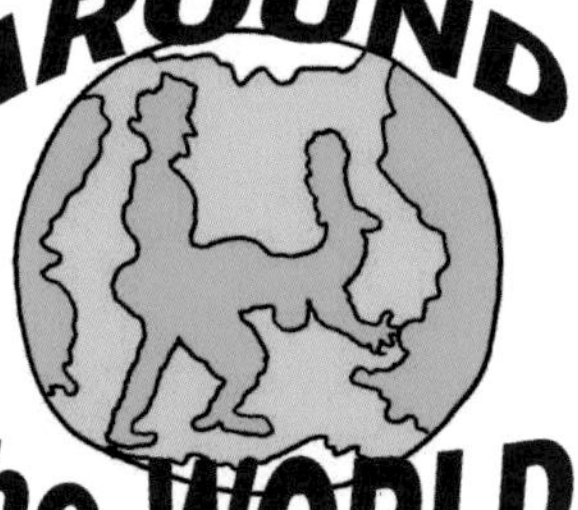

Sod the Olympics, the World Cup and Eurovision, the only thing that counts when determining world supremacy is how nifty a nation is at shagging...

The FRENCH!

Oh la laargh. They have to get pisséd on cheap red wine before gropies can even begin due to the excessive stench of garlic. Then they perform the National Dance of Foreplay – a disturbing striptease involving a beret, a garland of onions and a stale baguette... and all whilst balanced on a cronky bike with a basket on the front, yodelling "Oh-hi-oh-hi-oh". Nil points.

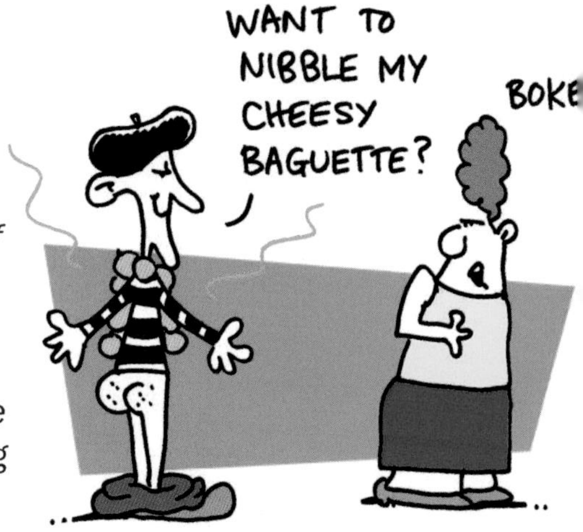
WANT TO NIBBLE MY CHEESY BAGUETTE?
BOKE

The ITALIANS!

The Romeos of the sex world? They spend so long talking and gesticulating about sex it's a wonder they ever get round to dipping the breadstick. When they finally do, they warble Rene and Renata's "Save Your Love" to each other, check their appearance in the mirror throughout, and shout "Mamma Mia" on climaxing. Then they escape this Italian Job on mini mopeds. Still, with all that spaghetti sucking, the women are very skilled at oral. Hmm, and the men provide their own sprinkling of Parmesan!

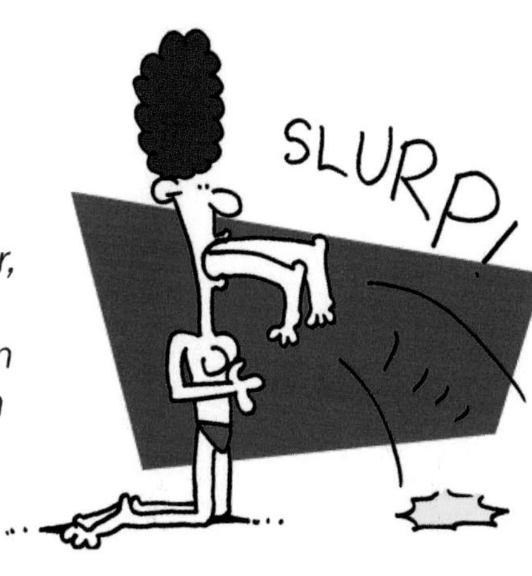
SLURP!

The IRISH!

What does 'the luck of the Irish' actually mean? It means you'll be lucky if you get jiggy in the (potato) sack with an Oirish person because they'll be paralytic. The only reason the shamrock's green is because it's got a hangover.

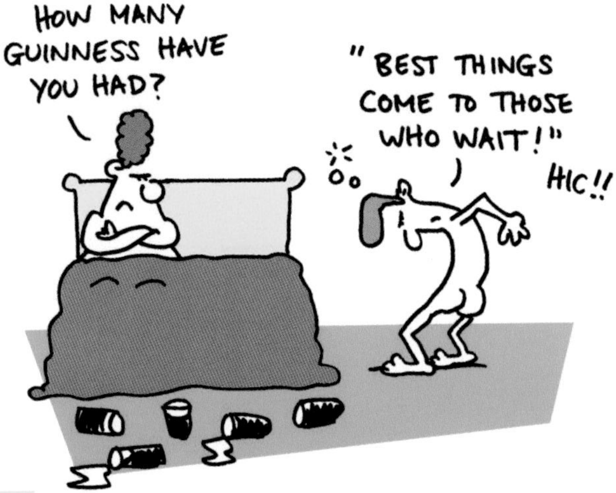
HOW MANY GUINNESS HAVE YOU HAD?
"BEST THINGS COME TO THOSE WHO WAIT!"
HIC!!

The SPANISH!

Latin lovers???! You'd think all those siestas would mean they'd spend the hot sexy afternoons playing "Let the Bull enter the Ring", but sex is on Spanish time – mañana! You see, Spaniards - as the world's hairiest race (yes, even more hairy than lesbians) - live in fear of sex as it may result in becoming permanently velcrosed together. That's why Spanish waiters go for English girls on holiday because once stuck to her pubic region, she'll have to bring him home to live unhappily ever after.

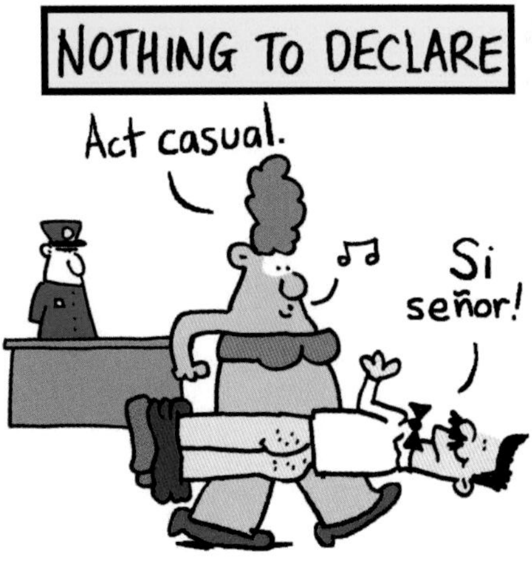
NOTHING TO DECLARE
Act casual.
Si señor!

The AMERICANS!

Just what is the American Dream? Freedom? Equality? Super-super-size? Nah. The dream is to be able to find their sex organs under those mountains of flab. That's why there's a virgin movement amongst their Teens. They can't find it to lose it!

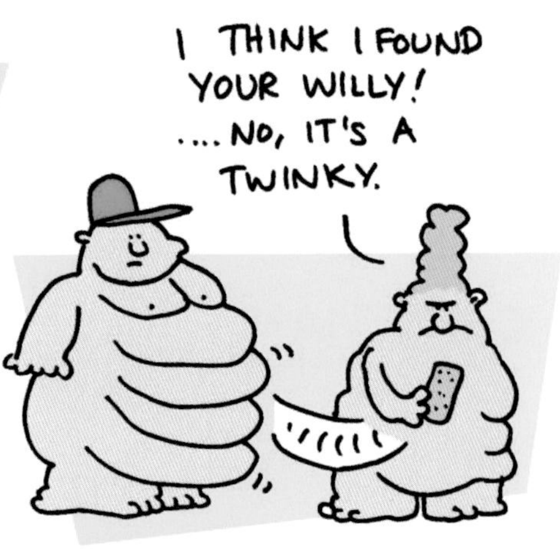
I THINK I FOUND YOUR WILLY! ....NO, IT'S A TWINKY.

SAUCY TRANSLATION GUIDE!

(OR HOW TO GET LAID IN ANY COUNTRY!)

Hey, who needs to know what "How much?", "Another beer please" or "I need to speak to the British Consulate NOW" are in a foreign language? Not us! The ONLY thing you need to know how to say is "DO YOU FANCY A SHAG?"

FRENCH
Voulez-vous avoir la filled baguette avec moi? Hoh-hee-hoh-hee...

AMERICAN
Wanna see if we can find our genitalia under this morbidly obese flesh, or get a burger?

DUTCH
Wil u rumpy pompy en sommige drugs mij hebben?

GERMAN
Wollen Sie Bratwurst sandwich mit mir haben?

MEXICAN
Si usted tiene sexo con mí, le pasaré de contrabando través de the border?

SCOTTISH
Gi'z the highland jig and I'll gi'ye a deep-fried pizza, Jimmy.

ITALIAN
Lei vuole avere il di Leaning Tower of Penis me?

RUSSIAN
Вы хотите иметь rumpy, качают меня. Mr Bond?

IRISH
Let's get another Guinness (hic) in first, then I'll show you me shamrock!

NORWEGIAN
Gjør De har rumpy-naturalblonde-pumpe vit meg?

WELSH
Would you like a Welsh rarebit, Mr Sheep?

CHRISTIAN
Let's wait till we get married to be disappointed.

(cut out and keep)

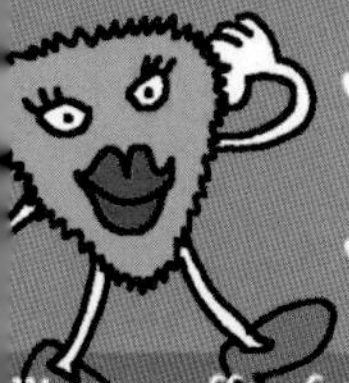

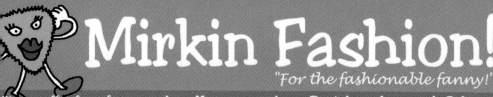

Mirkin Fashion!

"For the fashionable fanny!"

llions suffer from frumpy pubes. You are not alone. Don't be embarrassed. Pubes are respecter of age, race or celebrity status - even stars have crap pubes. They're just so manageable, impossible to straighten even with ceramics, and they don't take dye well k any ginger minger). What you need is a mirkin - a genital toupé. And because they me in lots of cool styles, you'll definitely want to show them off!

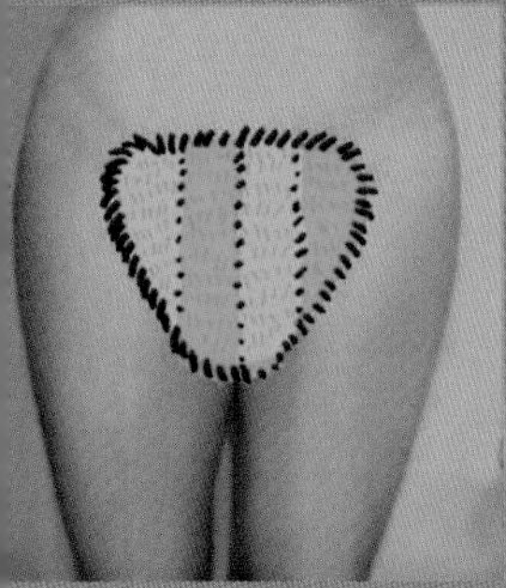

The Beckham
00% astroturf)

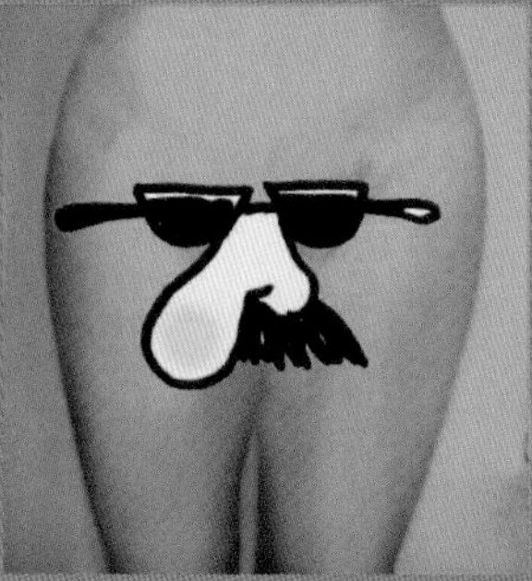

The Osama
Bin Laden

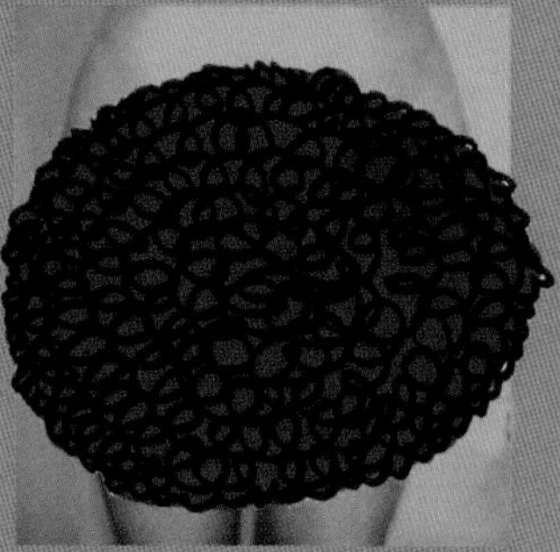

The Afro

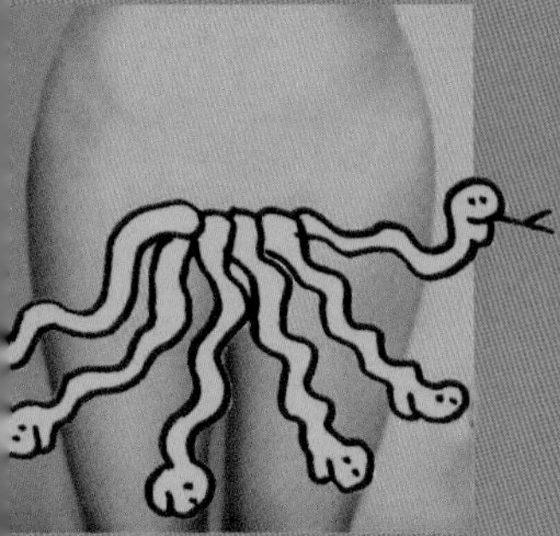

The Medusa

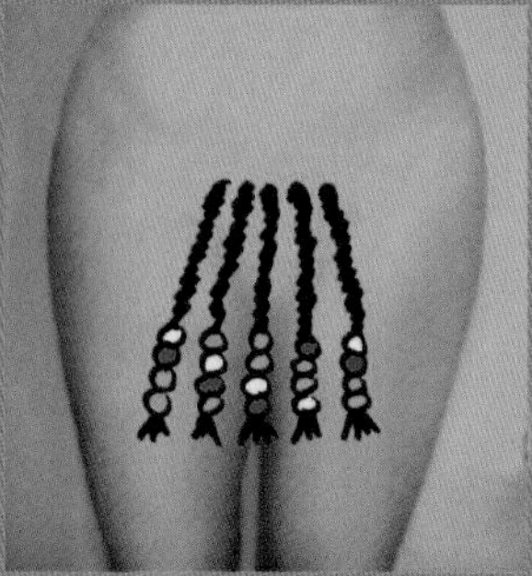

The Stevie Wonder

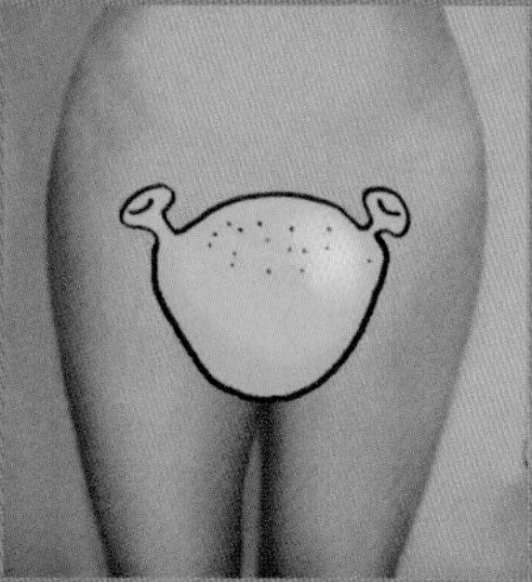

The Shrek

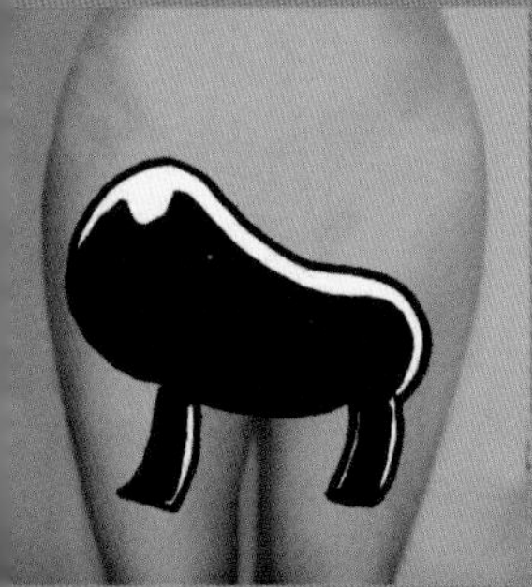

The Elvis

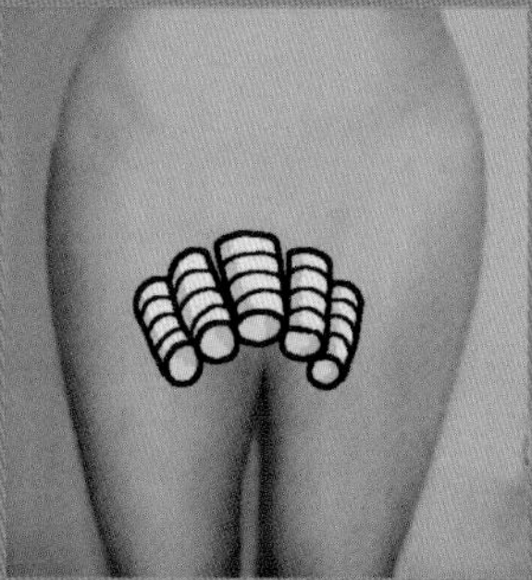

The Old Lady

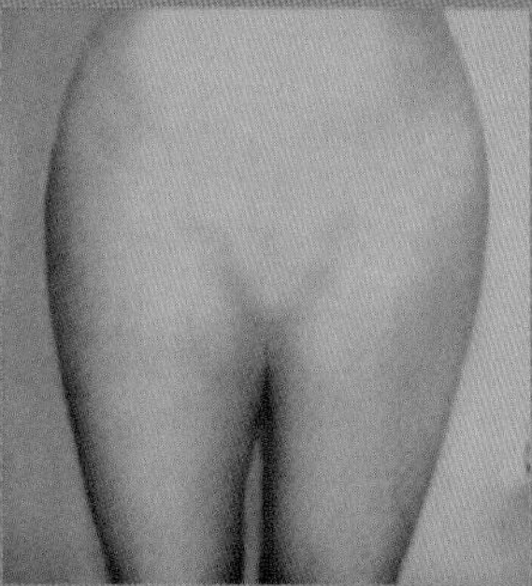

The Kojak

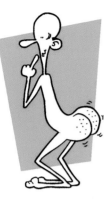

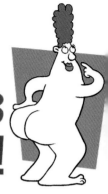

The DO's and DON'T's of HAVING SEX!

DO

USE LUBRICATION
AND BABY OIL!

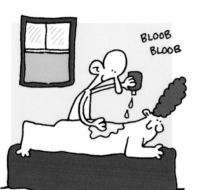

DON'T

USE TOO MUCH!

BLOOB
BLOOB

SLIP!

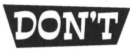

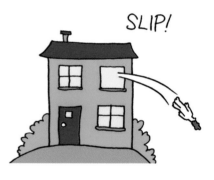

DO

TRY SEX
EQUIPMENT!

DON'T

LOSE THE
INSTRUCTIONS

OOOH!
CLIMB
IN!

PHONE
FOR
HELP!
I CAN'T
REACH!

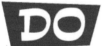

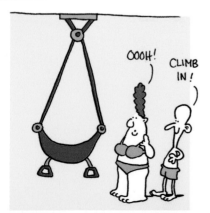

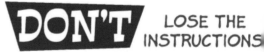

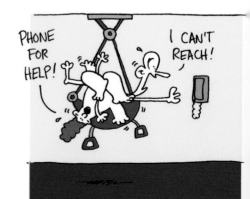

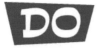

DO

COVER YOUR LOVER IN CHOCOLATE SAUCE AND WHIPPED CREAM!

YUM!

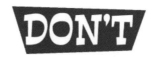

DON'T

GET CARRIED AWAY!

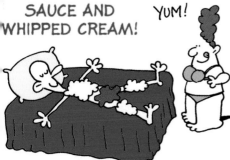

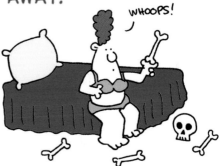

WHOOPS!

DO

HAVE SEX
N THE CAR!

BOING!
BOING!
B-DOING!

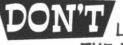

DON'T

LEAN ON THE HANDBRAKE!

OOH DARLING! I FEEL LIKE I'M FLYING!

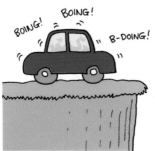

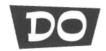

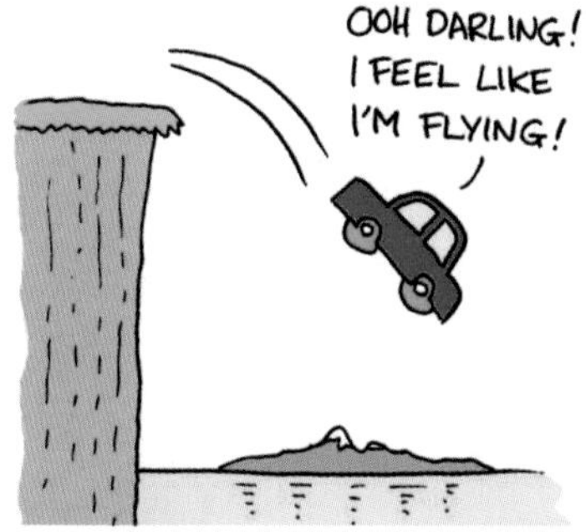

DO

HAVE SEX IN A PUBLIC TOILET!

OOH! NGG! NGGH!
Must be constipation

DON'T

HAVE A POO WHILE YOU'RE THERE!

AAAAAAAAAAAAAA!
I WAS BURSTING.
PLOP!

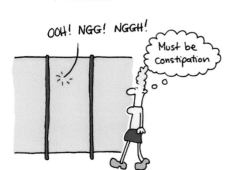

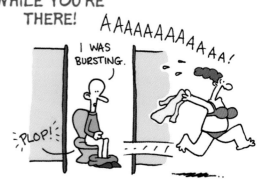

AN IDIOT'S GUIDE TO

Erogenous Zones

Don't risk ear nibbling (wax potatoes), toe sucking (stringy cheese) or back of knee sucking (varicose veins can be sucked through skin). It'll only result in unwanted calories. Besides, they don't work. In fact, the G-spot is an urban myth created by Woman to make the Male feel inadequate as they search for it. The real erogenous zones are far easier to find and arouse...

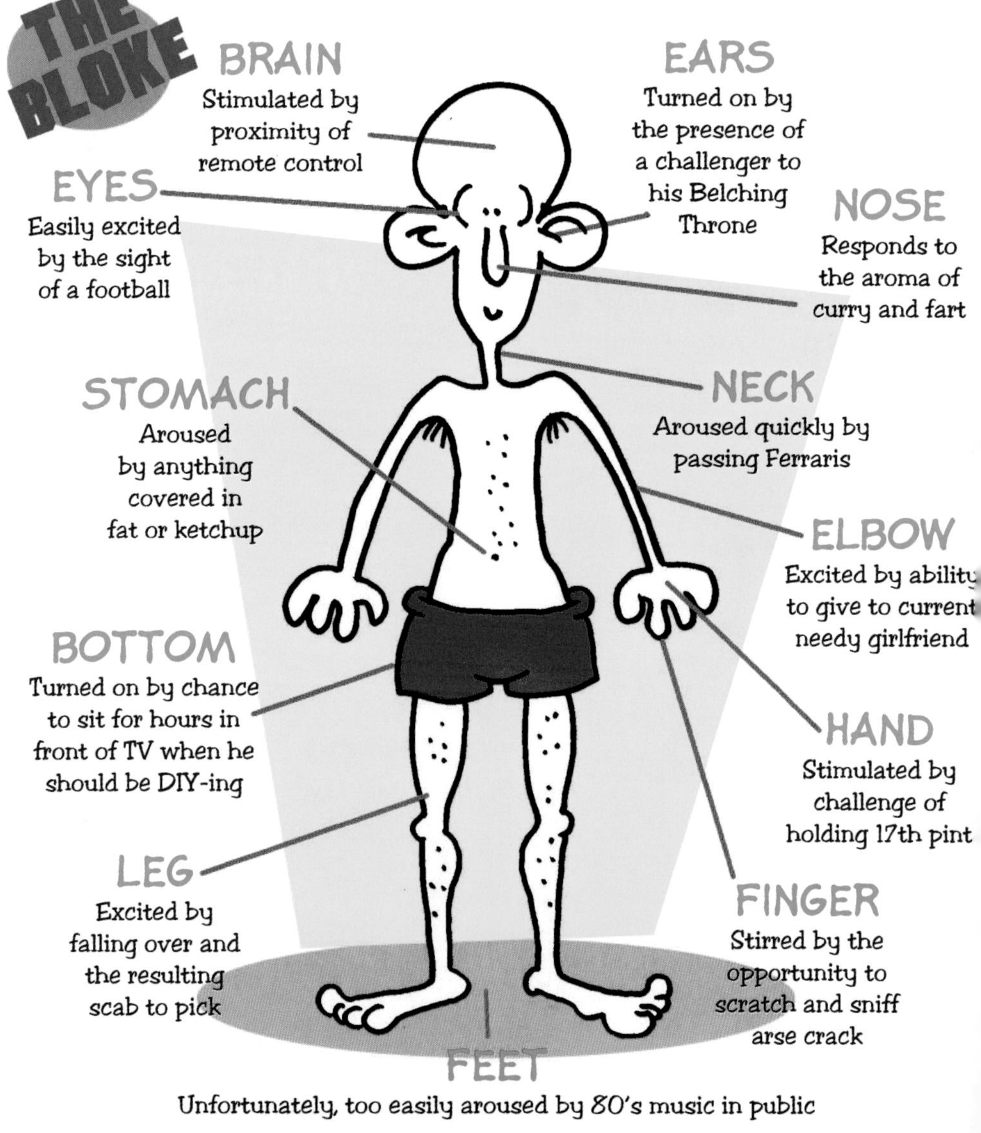

THE BLOKE
BRAIN
Stimulated by proximity of remote control
EARS
Turned on by the presence of a challenger to his Belching Throne
EYES
Easily excited by the sight of a football
NOSE
Responds to the aroma of curry and fart
STOMACH
Aroused by anything covered in fat or ketchup
NECK
Aroused quickly by passing Ferraris
ELBOW
Excited by ability to give to current needy girlfriend
BOTTOM
Turned on by chance to sit for hours in front of TV when he should be DIY-ing
HAND
Stimulated by challenge of holding 17th pint
LEG
Excited by falling over and the resulting scab to pick
FINGER
Stirred by the opportunity to scratch and sniff arse crack
FEET
Unfortunately, too easily aroused by 80's music in public

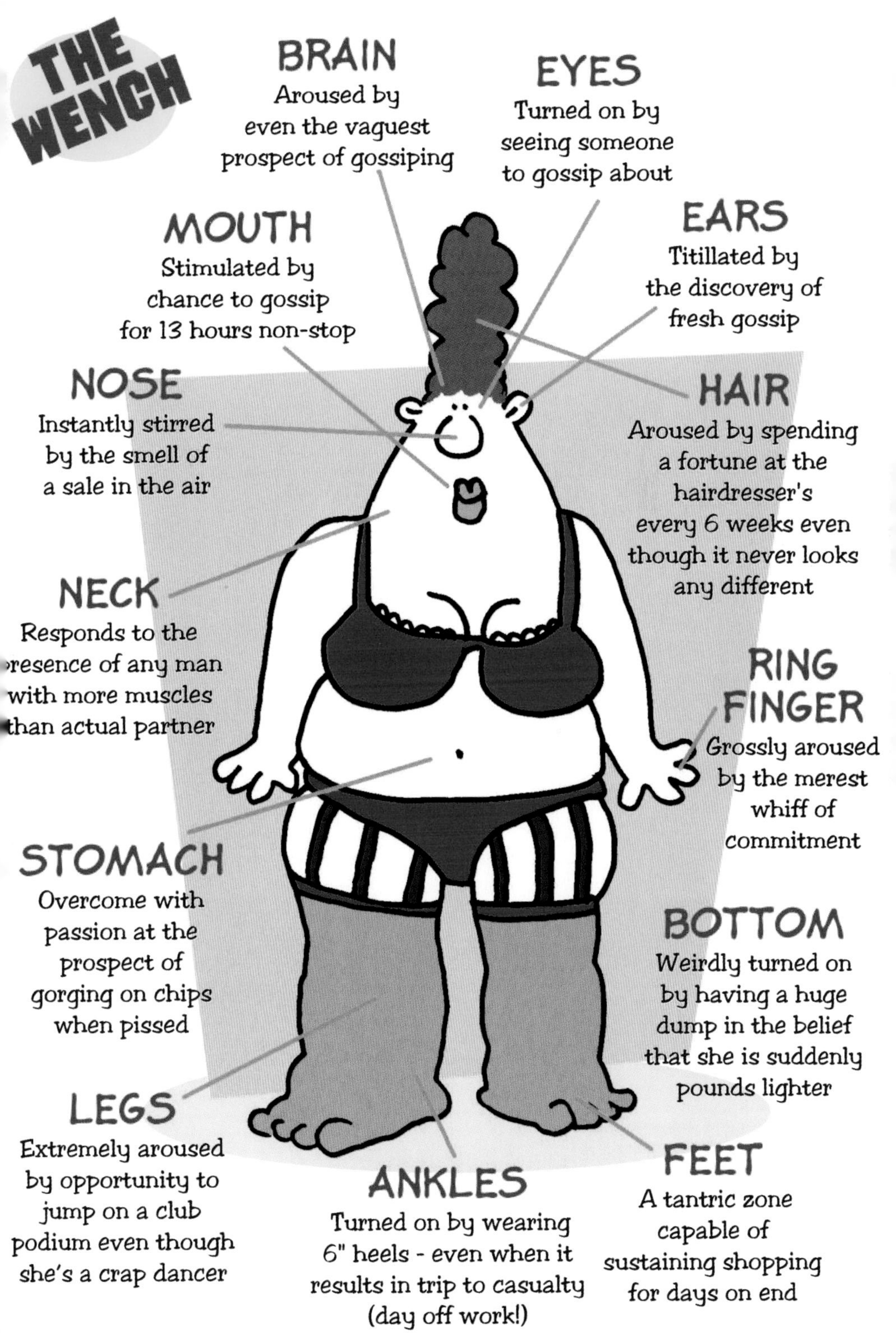
THE WENCH
BRAIN
Aroused by even the vaguest prospect of gossiping
EYES
Turned on by seeing someone to gossip about
MOUTH
Stimulated by chance to gossip for 13 hours non-stop
EARS
Titillated by the discovery of fresh gossip
NOSE
Instantly stirred by the smell of a sale in the air
HAIR
Aroused by spending a fortune at the hairdresser's every 6 weeks even though it never looks any different
NECK
Responds to the presence of any man with more muscles than actual partner
RING FINGER
Grossly aroused by the merest whiff of commitment
STOMACH
Overcome with passion at the prospect of gorging on chips when pissed
BOTTOM
Weirdly turned on by having a huge dump in the belief that she is suddenly pounds lighter
LEGS
Extremely aroused by opportunity to jump on a club podium even though she's a crap dancer
ANKLES
Turned on by wearing 6" heels - even when it results in trip to casualty (day off work!)
FEET
A tantric zone capable of sustaining shopping for days on end

THE MANY FACES OF WOMEN during SEX!

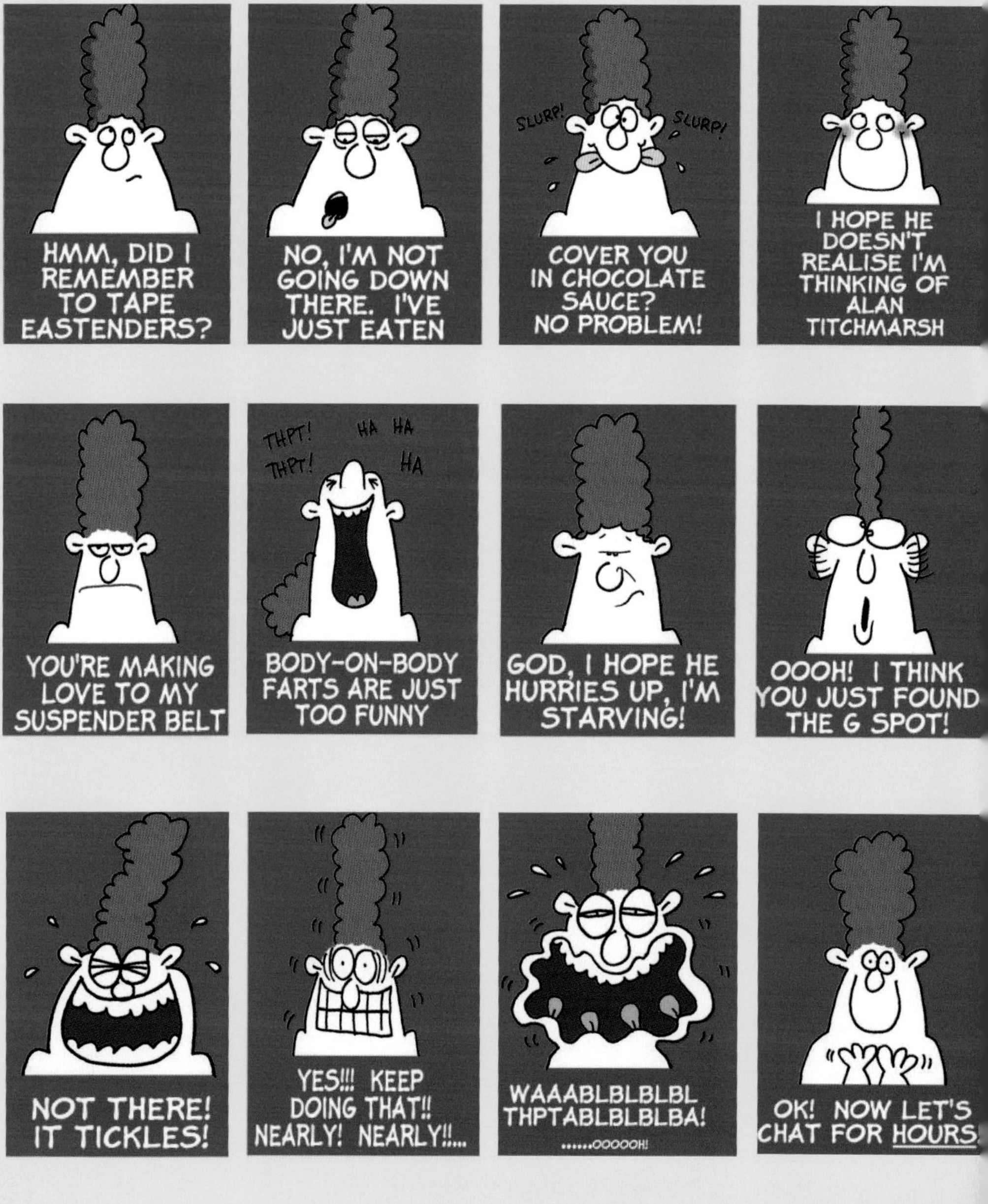
HMM, DID I REMEMBER TO TAPE EASTENDERS?
NO, I'M NOT GOING DOWN THERE. I'VE JUST EATEN
SLURP! SLURP!
COVER YOU IN CHOCOLATE SAUCE? NO PROBLEM!
I HOPE HE DOESN'T REALISE I'M THINKING OF ALAN TITCHMARSH
YOU'RE MAKING LOVE TO MY SUSPENDER BELT
THPT! THPT! HA HA HA
BODY-ON-BODY FARTS ARE JUST TOO FUNNY
GOD, I HOPE HE HURRIES UP, I'M STARVING!
OOOH! I THINK YOU JUST FOUND THE G SPOT!
NOT THERE! IT TICKLES!
YES!!! KEEP DOING THAT!! NEARLY! NEARLY!!...
WAAABLBLBLBL THPTABLBLBLBA!
......OOOOOH!
OK! NOW LET'S CHAT FOR HOURS!

The MANY FACES of MEN during SEX!

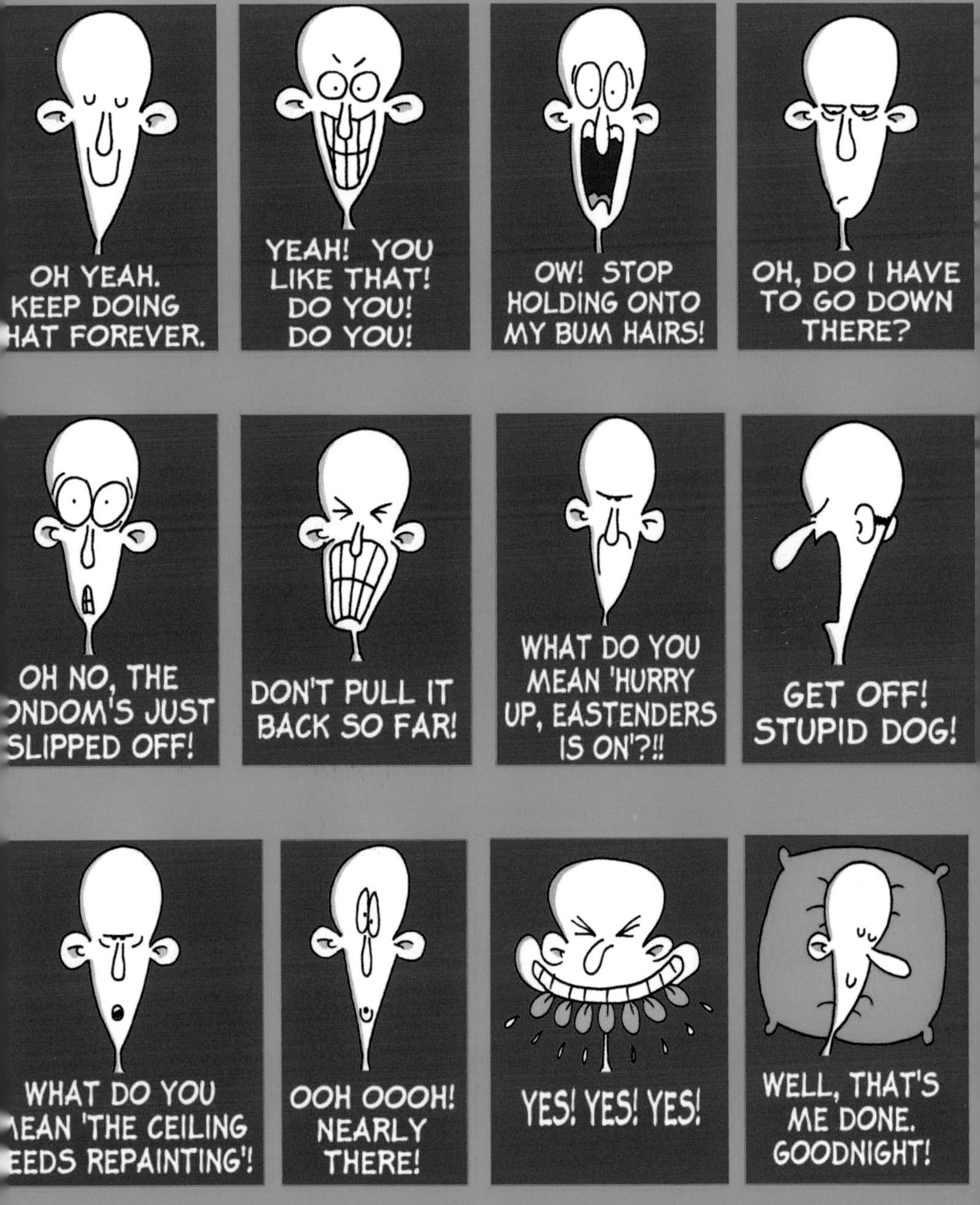

OH YEAH. KEEP DOING HAT FOREVER.
YEAH! YOU LIKE THAT! DO YOU! DO YOU!
OW! STOP HOLDING ONTO MY BUM HAIRS!
OH, DO I HAVE TO GO DOWN THERE?
OH NO, THE ONDOM'S JUST SLIPPED OFF!
DON'T PULL IT BACK SO FAR!
WHAT DO YOU MEAN 'HURRY UP, EASTENDERS IS ON'?!!
GET OFF! STUPID DOG!
WHAT DO YOU IEAN 'THE CEILING EEDS REPAINTING'!
OOH OOOH! NEARLY THERE!
YES! YES! YES!
WELL, THAT'S ME DONE. GOODNIGHT!

Some rather interesting facts about

SEX!

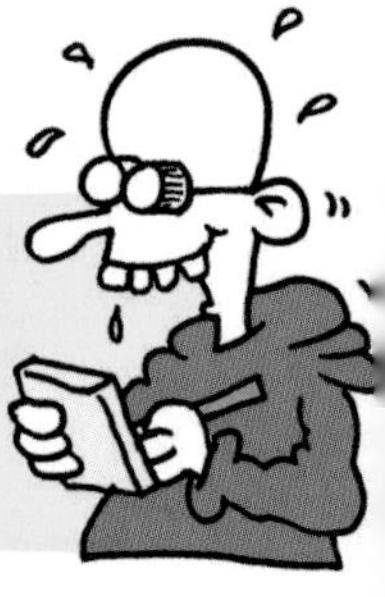

The average penis is 71% pork, 18% beef, 13% Gorgonzola, 2% cabbage, and 6.66% unfaithful.

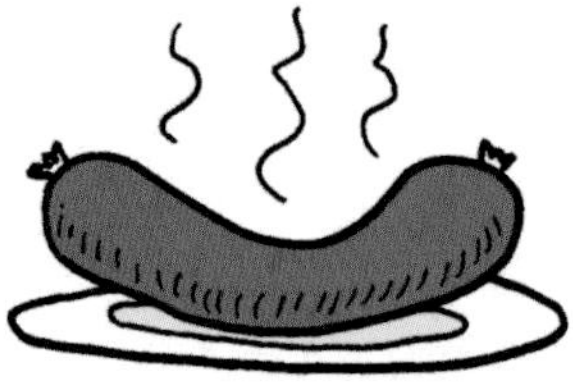

Women who live near radio station pylons can actually improve their radio reception by twiddling their nipples in an anti-clockwise direction.

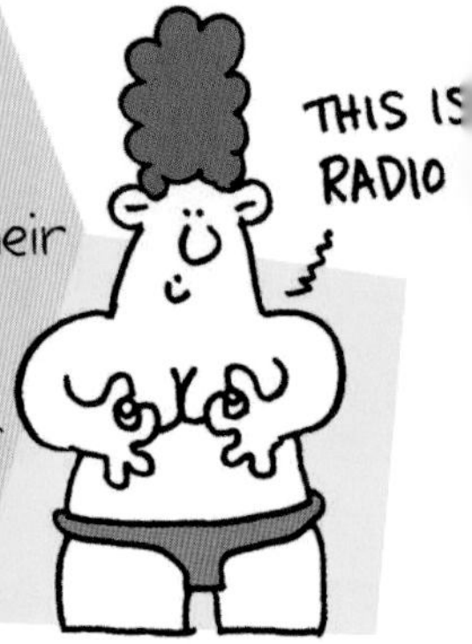
THIS IS
RADIO

Black men do not, in fact, have larger penises than white men. They simply walk around with huge magnifying screens in the gents to perpetuate the myth.

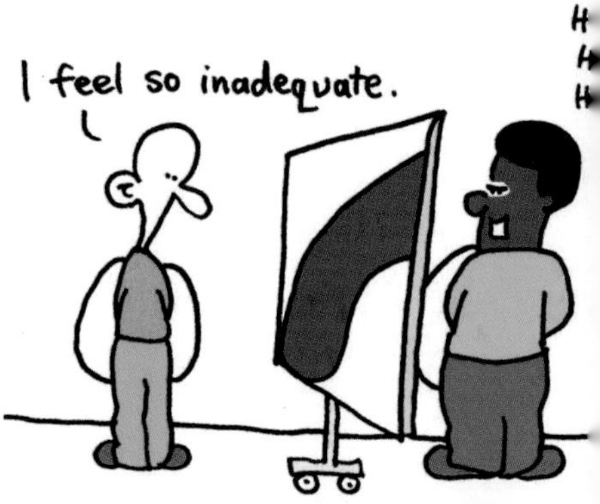
I feel so inadequate.

Pubic hair is actually naturally straight and only becomes curly when you eat bread crusts. Poker-straight pubies can be found in the cucumber-eating regions of Mayfair.

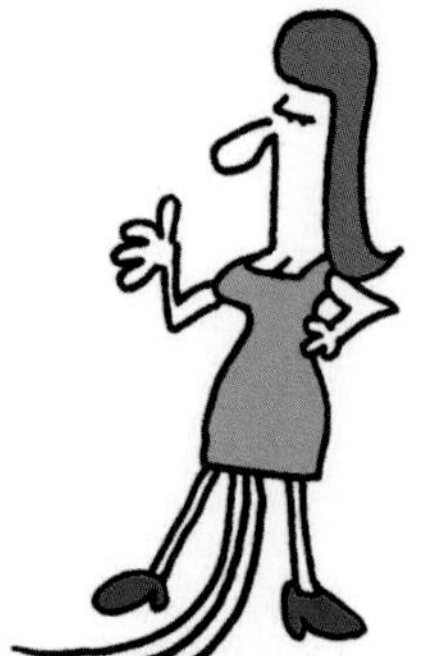

cohol does not cause brewer's droop. his is, in fact, the consequence of the male's emotional and psychological defences being dropped and the resulting realisation that the woman is a minger.

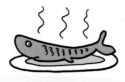

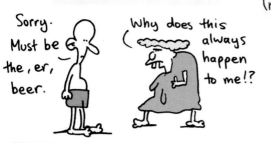

Sorry. Must be the, er, beer.
Why does this always happen to me!?

If the woman actually manages to climax before the male, there will be a puff of smoke and the man will be magically transformed into a pair of hoes. Unheard of in the western world.

POOF!

The average vagina is 83% hair, 28% frigid, 99% kipper, 0.003 promiscuous (rising to 67% in home counties) and 17% French.

It takes, on average, a man 12.6 minutes to successfully remove a bra, during which the woman has finished the washing up, done the dusting, picked her belly button fluff and put the rubbish out.

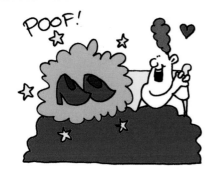

zz zzzz
I've done it!

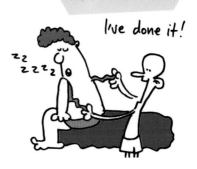

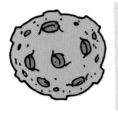

The average man's collection of porn laid end to end is exactly the same length as the skidmarks he collects in his pants over his lifetime - 273 km (that's here to the moon and back 27 times).

SEX GAMES!

(OR - FUN THINGS TO DO DURING BORING SEX!)

No matter how infrequently you have sex, it will often become incredibly tedious about half way through. These fun games will help you get through it. For one player or more. Age 13 and above

JOIN THE SPOTS!

Ideal for doggie-style positions, simply take a permanent marker or tattoo kit and connect the zits to reveal the picture within. Have even more fun by not telling your partner what you're up to. Hee hee.

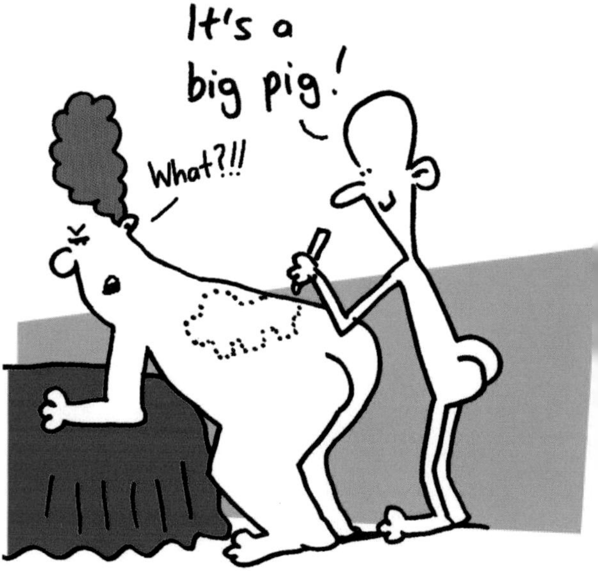

It's a big pig!
What?!!

COUNT THE SHOES!

This game is also very adaptable to many other boring situations: job interviews, performing life-saving surgery if a doctor, or at weddings and funerals. Men may wish to substitute the shoes for lager, whilst the gays can play with leather caps and moustaches.

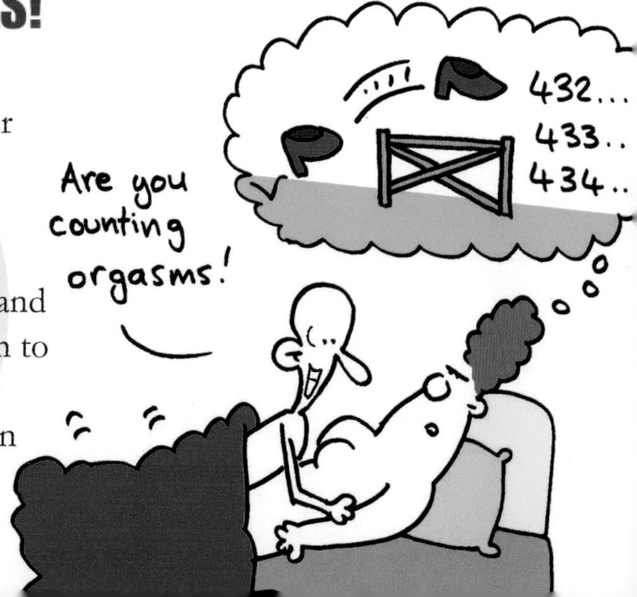

432...
433...
434...
Are you counting orgasms!

MEMORISE THE STAINS!

For advanced players only. Study the stains on the bedsheets, then the next time they're washed (which can be anywhere between 1 week for repressed female, and 14 months if a single male) see if you can remember where the old stains were.

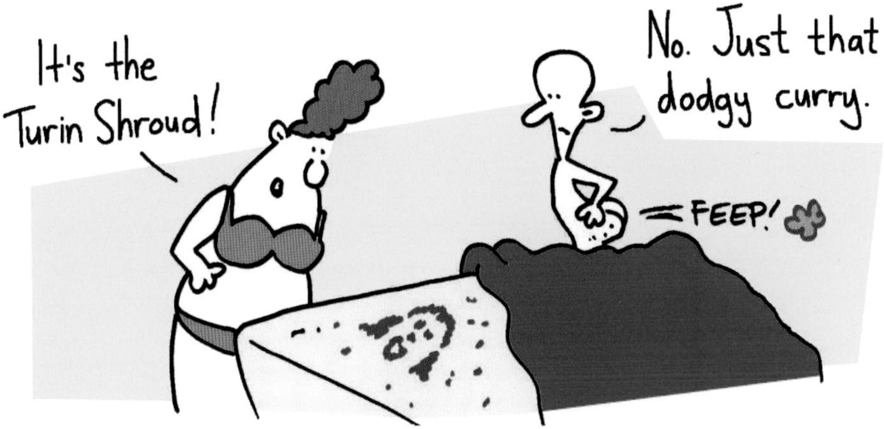

It's the Turin Shroud!
No. Just that dodgy curry.
FEEP!

READY, STEADY, COOK!

Having sex can make you very hungry – after all, the average couple expends 3 calories per hour in the missionary position. So, gather all the crumbs in your bed and see what kind of snack you can improvise out of the ingredients. Yum.

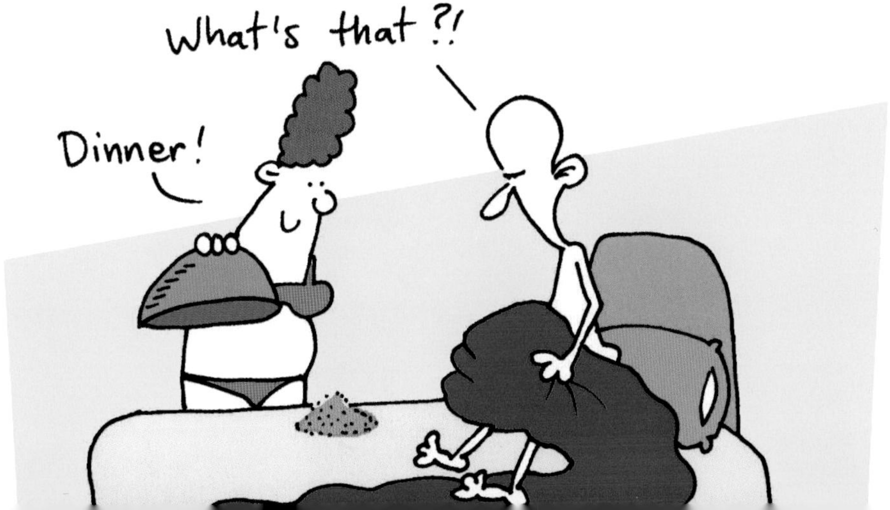

What's that?!
Dinner!

KNIT THE NOSE HAIR!

This is a great game for the winter months when it's a bit chilly – the only limit is your imagination: scarves, hats, gloves, fur coats…

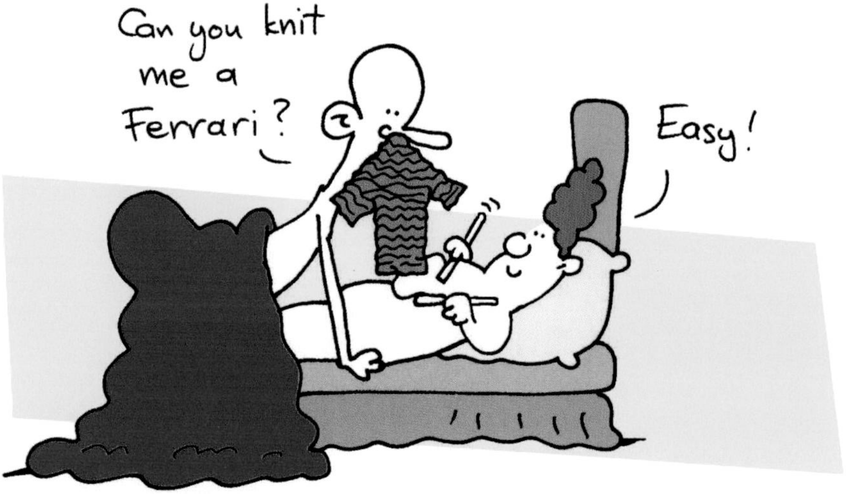
Can you knit me a Ferrari?
Easy!

VENTRILOQUISM!

The mouth can get particularly bored during sex as most couples don't bother with kissing after a couple of minutes. So, instead of shouting sexual instructions or discussing how to redo the bedroo décor, play tricks on each other by practising throwing your voice.

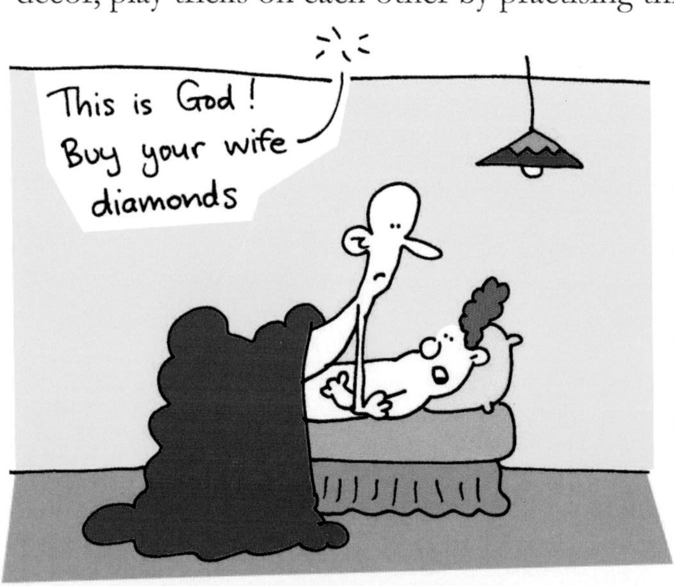
This is God! Buy your wife diamonds

SUGGESTIONS:

a) "This is the police! You're surrounde
b) "Cooey, it's your Mum"
c) "Your money or your wife!"
d) "We come in Peace

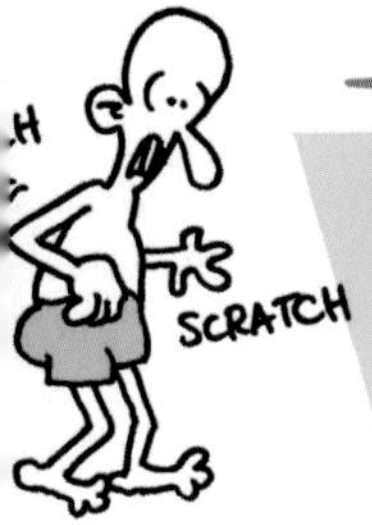
SCRATCH

The Horrible World of SEX DISEASES!

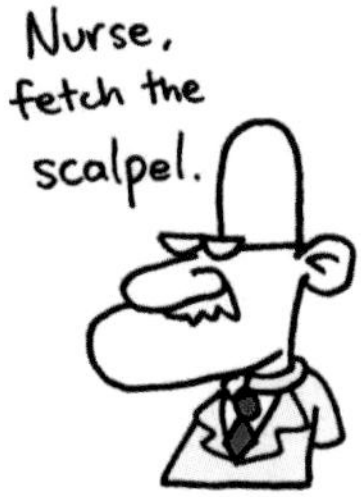
Nurse, fetch the scalpel.

VD is the tip of the itchy iceberg. There's a whole range of STDs that re both deadly, highly contagious, but, more worryingly, EMBARRASSING. Horrible things your parents never told you about. Sods. They WANTED you to catch them...

GONTOBEDEARLEA

'he modern-day plague of the long-term relationship. Particularly ontagious amongst women and gays in straight relationships.

YMPTOMS:

nclude a rash decision to go to bed early, leaving the randy male eeling sore, knowing that to wake her means certain death. Further ymptoms include snoring, bad pyjamas, whilst the male will suffer a alloused but happy hand.

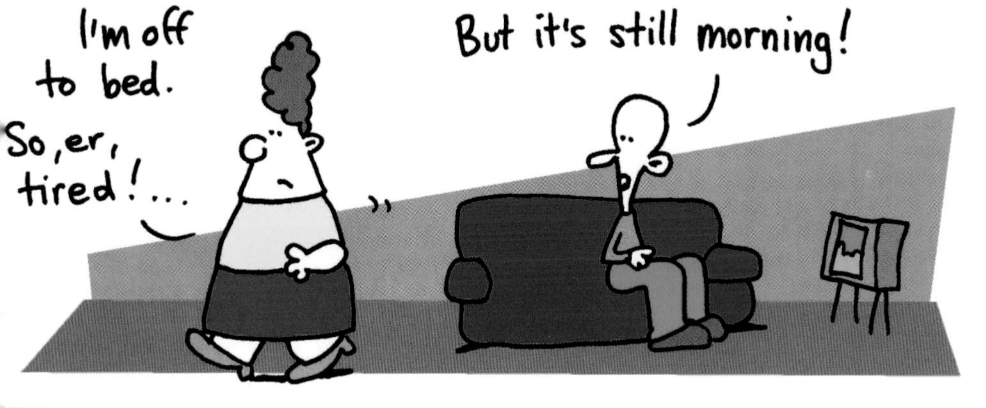
I'm off to bed.
So, er, tired!...
But it's still morning!

REATMENT:

A liberal application of wine and chocolate to the afflicted female at pproximately 7pm when there's nothing much on the telly, followed y a huge dose of flattery should result in a temporary return of emale libido. Ultimately, though, this condition is incurable.

BURPEES

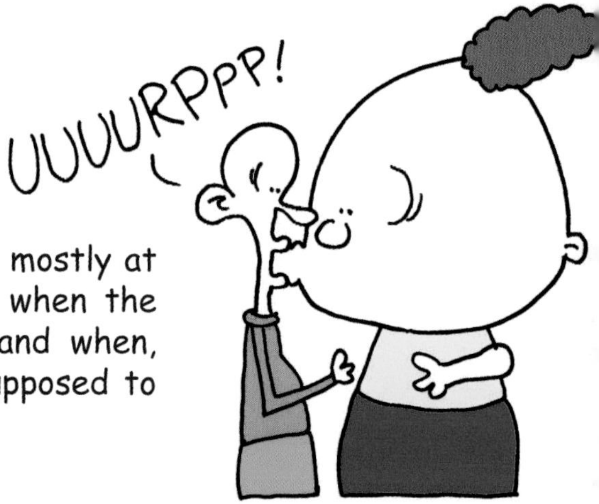
UUUURPPP!

A common condition afflicting all men and some gutter women. It strikes its victims down mostly at weddings and christenings when the booze (hic) is (hic) free and when, usually, such events are supposed to result in drunken sex.

SYMPTOMS:

Include uncontrollable, violent eruptions of (hic) belching - ofte accompanied by the unpleasant side effects of the aroma o stomach contents (for men that means curry, kebab and lager; fo women it means the much more heinous stench of vegetables). Thi is followed by childish bouts of annoying giggling. In very rar cases, the victim may be able to belch the entire alphabet - contac the Guinness Book of Records immediately.

TREATMENT:

There is no known cure. A natural remedy is **not** to drop a key dow their back, but to apply a quick slap to the side of their head whe symptoms persist.

SELFISHILIS

A plague of biblical proportions, striking males down from an early age. Also known as Spankus Monkious or Bashious Bishopus.

SYMPTOMS:

Look for the external signs first - guilty faces, locked doors, soggy tissues, magazines "hidden" in his sock drawer, calloused palms, a satisfied and serene smile, cheerfulness, uncharacteristic generosity, twinkle in eye, compliments, hand washing... The diagnosis is simple - he's been pleasuring himself.

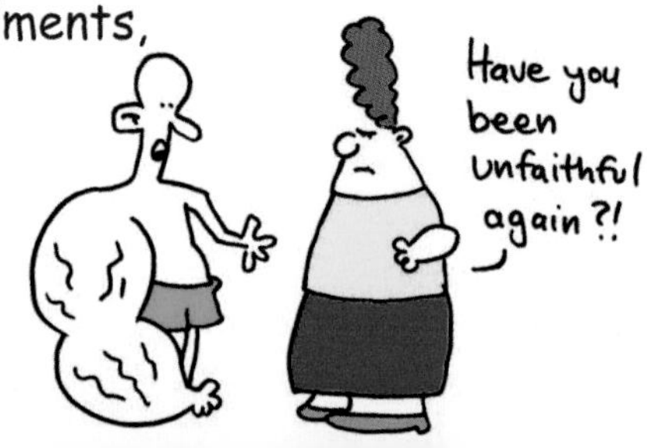
Have you been unfaithful again?!

TREATMENT: Forget it!

HAIRYITIS BE

fatal disease afflicting
omen, increasing with age or
hange in sexual orientation.

I think it's time to do your bikini line.

YMPTOMS:
ook out for the terminal
eglect of shaving, particularly
he shocking loss of interest
ruining your shaver. Afflicted areas include legs, armpits,
onobrow, bikini line (line!?!.. shouldn't that be hedge?), base of back,
op lip and toes. Sadly, this ailment will result in termination of male
esire – he might as well be doing it with a bloke.

REATMENT:
pply liberal dose of verbal humiliation in public. If this shaming does
ot result in immediate defuzzing, you must seek private treatment –
head to toe salon wax. Or dump her – it's cheaper.

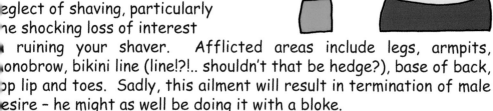

GLAM-MISSES-HER

gh. It's a miracle the human race manages to survive with this
ontagion of the 21st Century threatening male desire to procreate
ith the female species.

YMPTOMS:
physically repulsive
isease... a normal healthy
lam appearance is slowly
eplaced by big knickers,
aggy bras that were
hite 12 years ago,
ismatched pants and
ras, pop socks and vests.

Come and get it big boy!

No thanks!

REATMENT:
ttempt to apply a generous dose of matching sexy underwear.
ot that it'll work. Women seem to perversely enjoy their affliction.
lternative treatment suggestion: take a younger lover.

Can you give me a home?

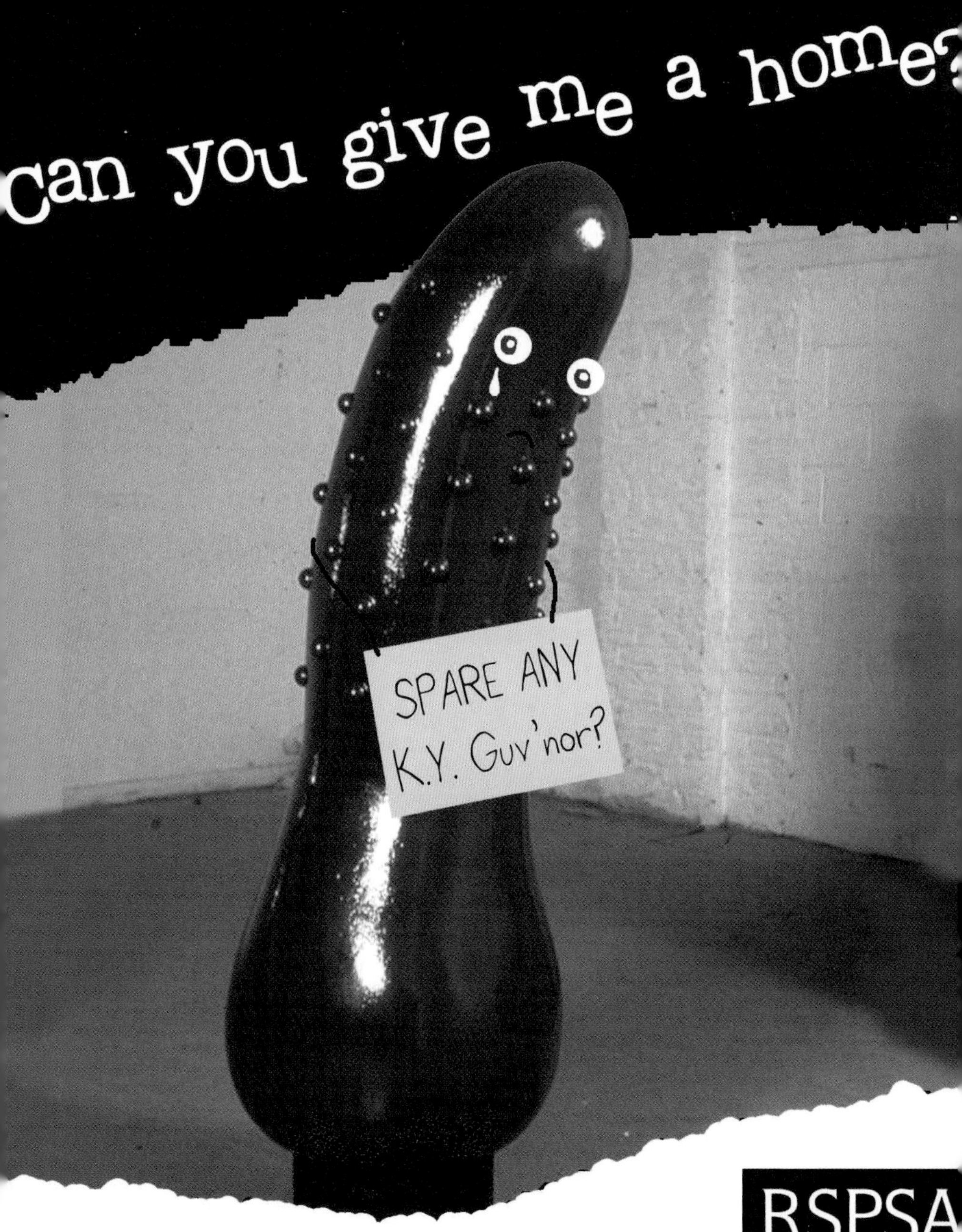
SPARE ANY
K.Y. Guv'nor?

Every year, thousands of innocent sex toys are left cold and alone, deprived of human physical contact and emotional warmth, and stuffed callously in dark drawers, wardrobes and under mattresses. The RSPSA aims to find them new, caring homes – if you think you could adopt a Sex Aid, please send £3,000 to Swizz Bank Account 666 666 NOW to cover admin' costs. Remember to disinfect before use. Unless you're a lesbian hoping for free artificial insemination.

RSPSA

The Royal Society for the Protection of Sex Aids

Spreading Love
Spreading Legs

The Odd Squad Guide to SEX AFTER MARRIAGE

REAL LIFE SEX-AIDS!

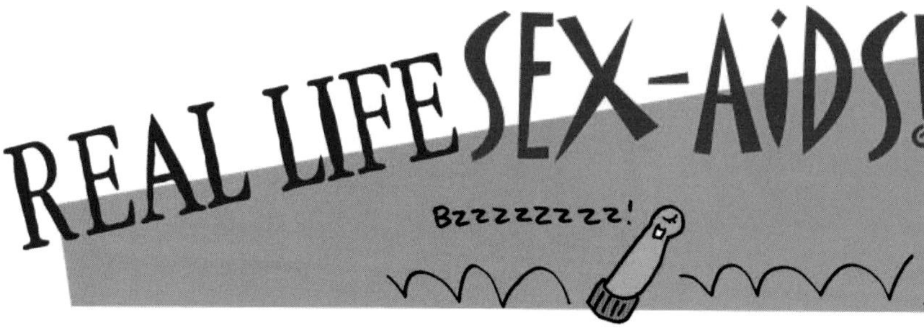
Bzzzzzzzz!

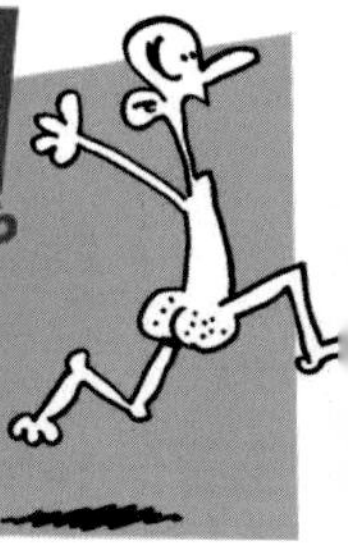

Stuff your dildos, inflatable dolls and vibrators. Only female PE teachers and librarians actually use them. These are the sex aids used in millions of homes, bushes, car seats and the back of bike-sheds throughout the land. Well, maybe not millions. Only 352 homes in the UK - including your parents' - actually have regular rumpy...

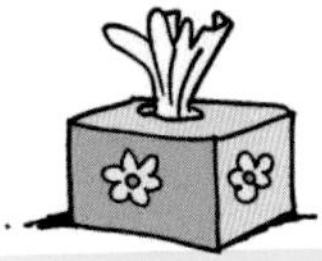

TISSUES

Previously the domain of the single, slightly strange male, the tissue is now vital equipment for all sex-makers. Younger couples will favour hastily torn pieces from the toilet's loo roll - probably after sex by the screaming woman. In fact, some women actually leg it for the tissue even before sperm blast-off. Whilst older, stagnant couples whose passion is mis-spent co-ordinating textiles will prefer a decorative box of tissues on the matching bedside table (though, truth be told, the tissues will only ever be used for mopping up their secret tears). NB, if tissues aren't to hand (or, as revenge, if man discharges on skin or sheet) the woman will use his discarded underwear. He'll put them back on afterwards.

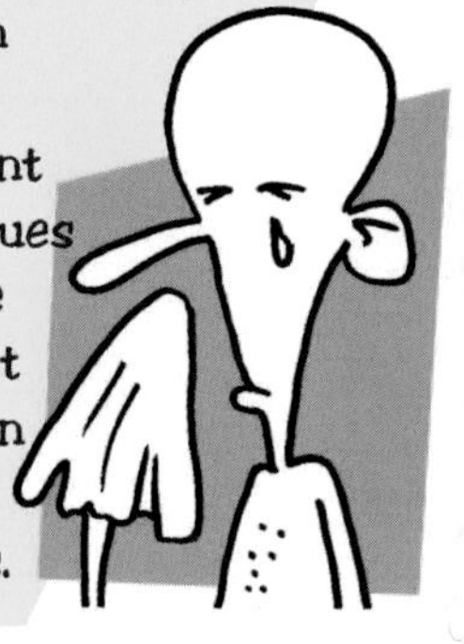

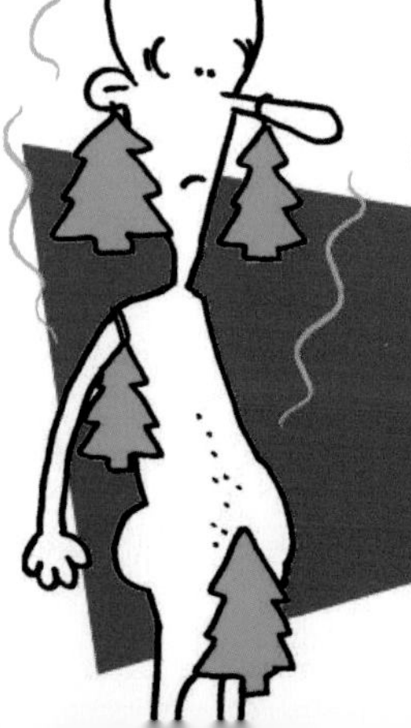

AIR FRESHENER

Sex stinks. Both (or all) of you. So, spray the air mid-climax to help masque the stench of rotting food items, then, for added fun, have a race to the shower. The loser has to redecorate the boudoir to eliminate the stench that has already impregnated the wallpaper, carpet and curtains.

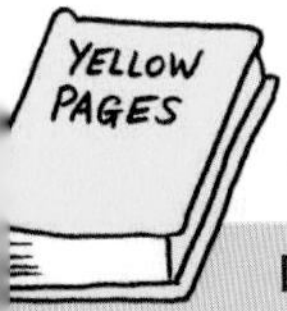
YELLOW PAGES

A GOOD BOOK

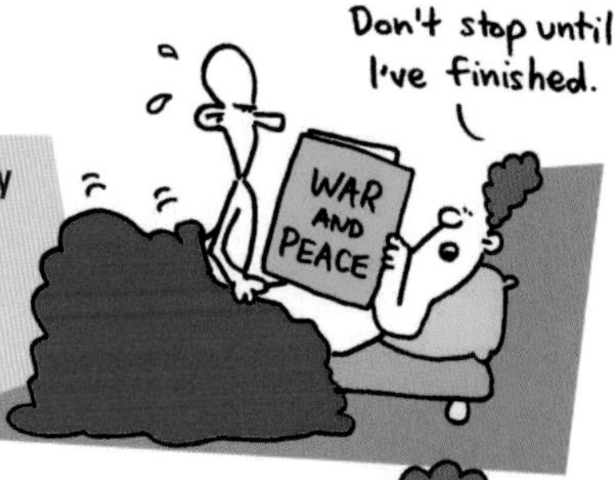
Don't stop until I've finished.
WAR AND PEACE

Don't start sex without one. At any oint from foreplay to climax (yes, any time in hose three minutes), either party may become ored soft by the goings-on. A thick epic will erve as a welcome distraction.

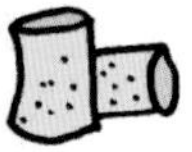

EAR PLUGS

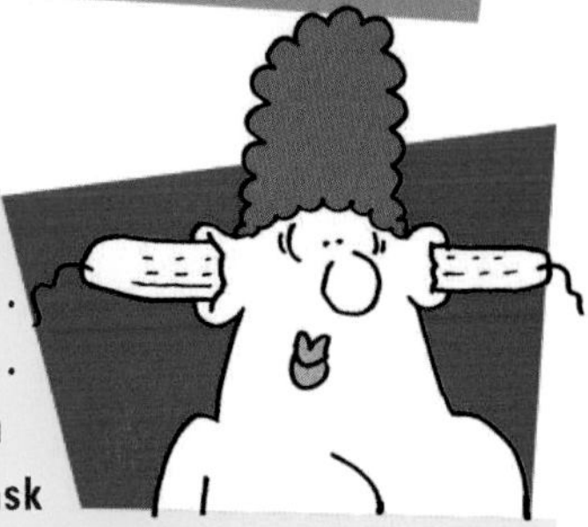

ugh. No-one likes listening to dirty talk - it's ff-putting, unintentionally hilarious and pretentious. hilst moaning and groaning smacks of self-centredness. f proper earplugs aren't available, collect bogey jam or 3-4 weeks and mould artistically to fit (why not ask riends for donations?). Alternatively, insert tampons in both ears (heavy low variety is ideal). It's a scientific fact that Van Gogh actually cut off is ear whilst he was bedding a compulsive chatter (he'd have cut off the other ar but, like many, he was addicted to cotton buds). Married couples may enjoy eaving earplugs in permanently to avoid listening to nagging or football or owel/consonant sounds.

BEER GOGGLES

Quite frankly, it'd be reckless to begin sex without this invaluable sex aid. Young or old, single or unfaithful, employed or state-scrounger, gay or repressed, beer goggles guarantee you a good time. Until the morning after.

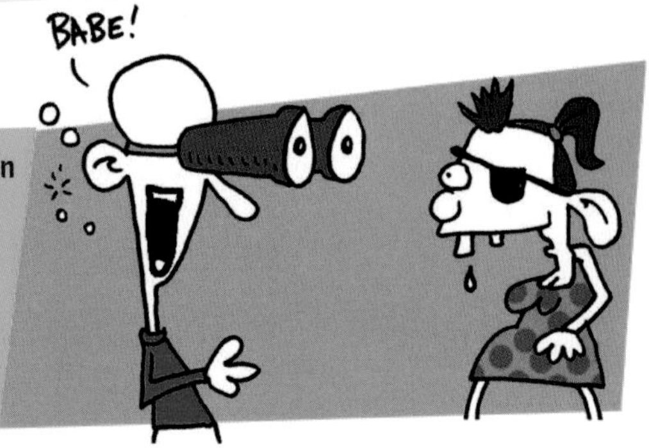
BABE!

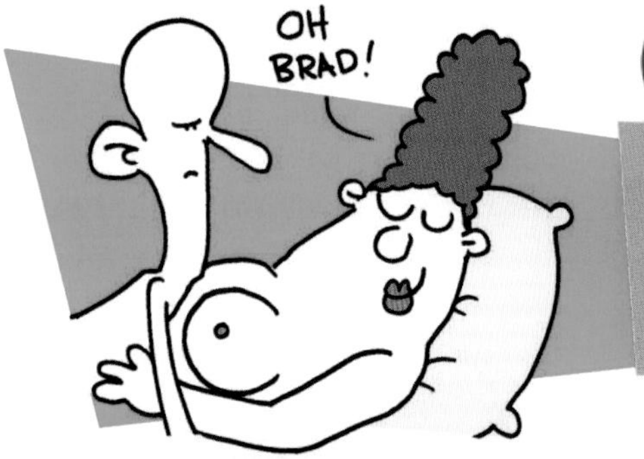
OH BRAD!

EYELIDS

A much under-rated sex aid. Simply close your eyes to increase sexual desire and satisfaction. Remember not to peak. It'll ruin it.

ALTERNATIVE USES FOR SEX TOYS!

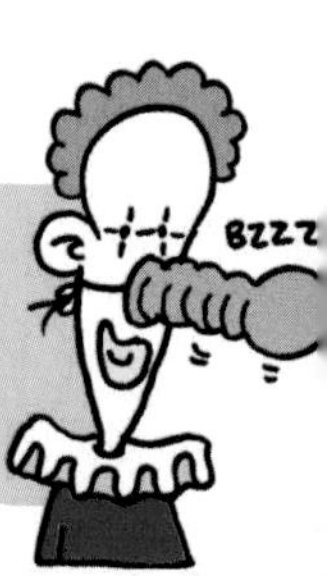
BZZZ

Pretend all you like that it was your friends who bought your sex toys for a stag do/hen weekend/birthday/funeral or whatever... lacy pants on fire! We all know YOU did. And now you're too ashamed, embarrassed, or thick to use them. Now they're gathering dust in your drawers for your mum to find them (yup, no matter how old you are, she still rifles through your stuff). So unless you're prepared to give them up to a more loving home (eg. Help the Aged) then follow these wholesome suggestions for alternative uses...

THE INFLATABLE SEX DOLL!

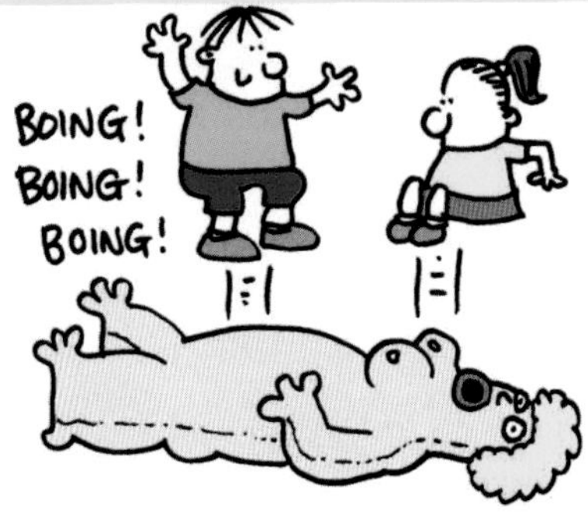
BOING!
BOING!
BOING!

This sex toy, Rosy, is most versatile: in th summer months you can hire her out as a sma and affordable bouncy castle for sma underdeveloped children (inner city variety) a local fetes. Or, young and old alike can enjo using Rosy as a floating aid in the pool or at th seaside (warning - beware of denture punctures

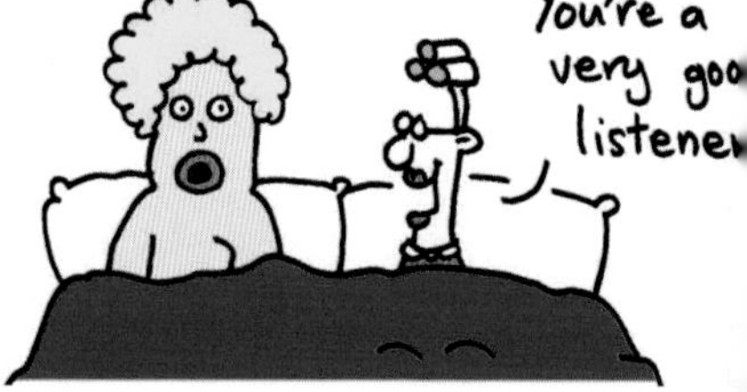
You're a very goo listene

Whilst in the winter, Rosy makes a great draught excluder for poor, old people. Or, as a substitute partner when the other half snuffs it due to pneumonia. Old folk can also use Rosy - deflated - as an incontinence sheet - either on the bed or tied like a nappy.

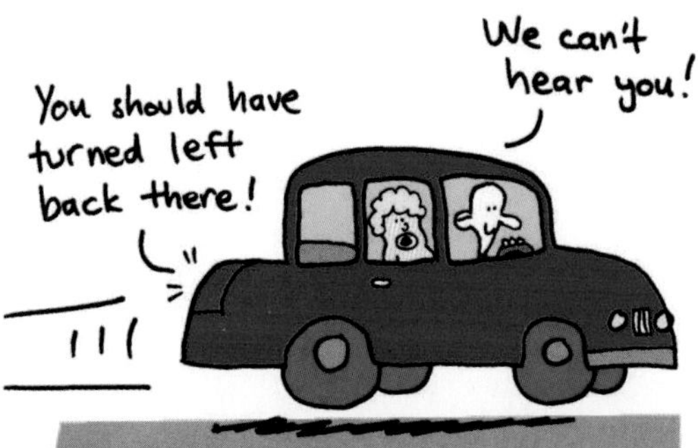
You should have turned left back there!
We can't hear you!

Alternatively, single women may als benefit from using Rosy as a mal dummy in the car to deter roadsid psychos hiding in bushes or the eve more disturbing phenomenon, va drivers (tip: to turn Rosy into convincing male, add a trilby an position hands in the air as if i despair at female driving). Men ma also enjoy a similar use - as a non nagging female car companio (suggestion: put your real partner i the boot).

THE RUBBER DILDO!

All men feel emotionally and physically more secure if they know there are sausages in the fridge. Avoid potential tantrums by attaching several dildos together with tampon string and keep in fridge as a sausage security blanket (idea: if you only have one dildo, why not pretend it's an impressive German saveloy!).

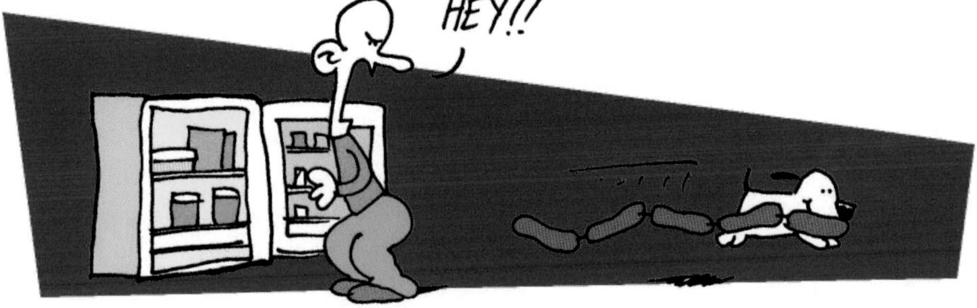
HEY!!

Alternatively, children can use the dildo as a rolling pin when making cookies (hint: perhaps wash dildo first). Or, save on extortionate tickets to Ten Pin Bowling Alleys by getting together with friends, neighbours and strangers to use your dildos as bowling pin substitutes (suggestion: use the worst player's severed head as bowling ball). Only gays and lesbians have enough dildos to make their own alley.

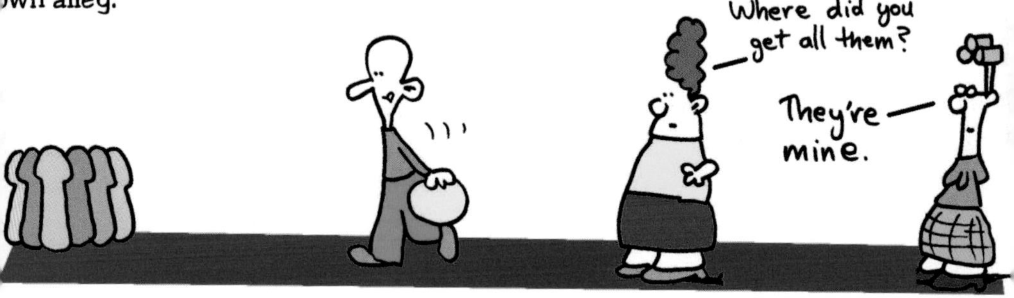
Where did you get all them?
They're mine.

And, should you own a black dildo, why not give to an elderly relative as a walking cane. Paint it white and you can use it to skip queues at theme parks, sports events, everywhere!

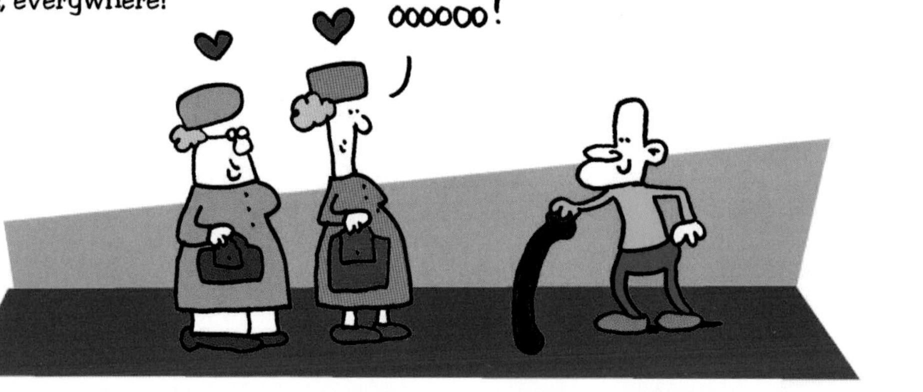
oooooo!

THE VIBRATOR!

Babies will love the womb-like soothing effect of the vibrations, and the hum is a far more pleasing lullaby than the mother's dreadful caterwaulings. Plus, it doesn't pull crap, psyche-scarring faces.

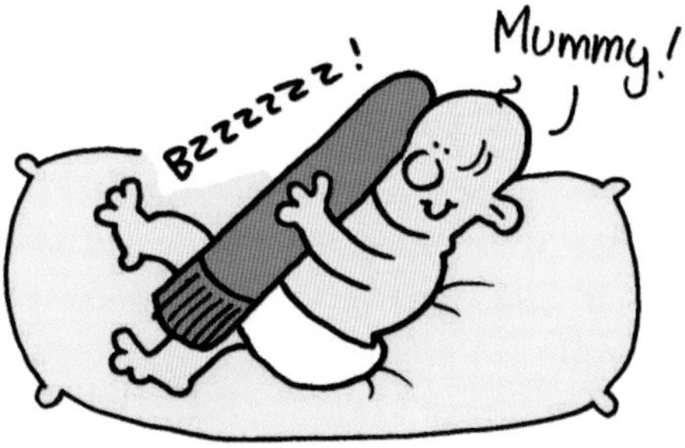
Bzzzzzz!
Mummy!

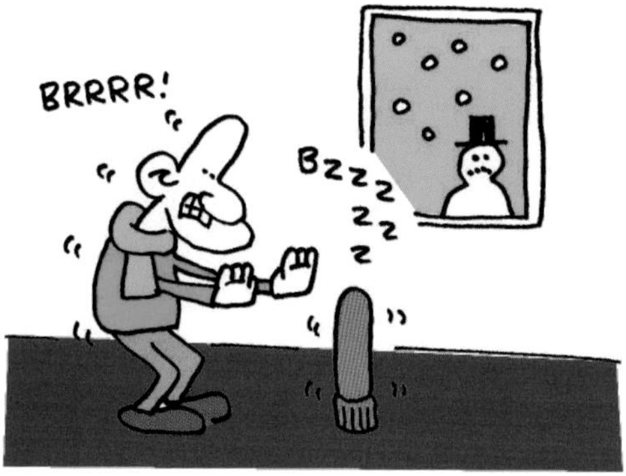
BRRRR!
Bzzzzzz

Old people can supplement their heatin expenses by using the friction from th vibrations to create a heat source. (Tip: if they leave it on long enough they can also use it to heat up thei dinner of own-brand beans).

Women, why not use your vibrators as a cost-effective. alternative abs-belt. Tie together and wear discreetly throughout the day. (NOTE: on second thoughts, this idea is genius and will have been patented by the illustrious "authors" of this great masterpiece. It's OURS! OURS!!)

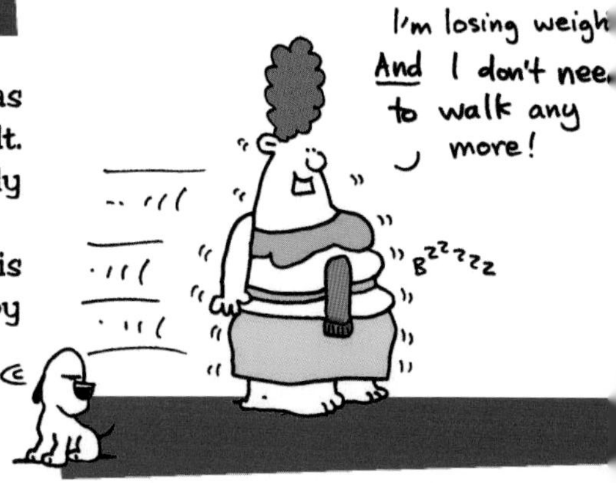
I'm losing weigh And I don't nee to walk any more!
Bzzzzz

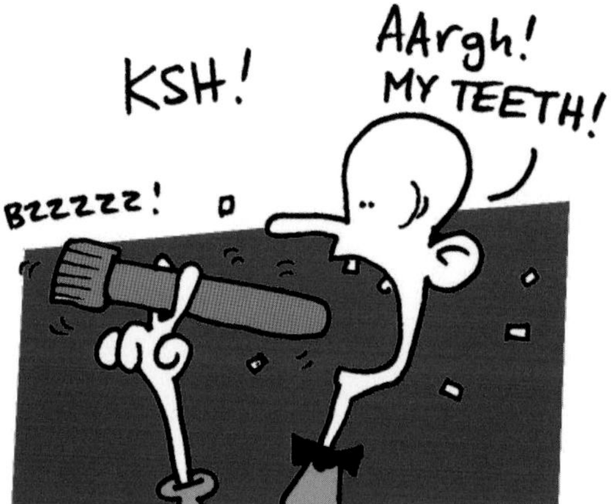
KSH!
AArgh! MY TEETH!
Bzzzzz!

Men! Now you need never get caught short at wedding receptions around midnight when all the real men pull out their cigars. Boy, will they be jealous of your ever-lasting "Cuban".

KINKY HANDCUFFS!

Women, the best alternative use of handcuffs is to lock your man to whatever DIY job he's been saying he'll do for months. Lure him to the scene by telling him you're wearing that tacky red basque he bought you. Gullible fool! As if!

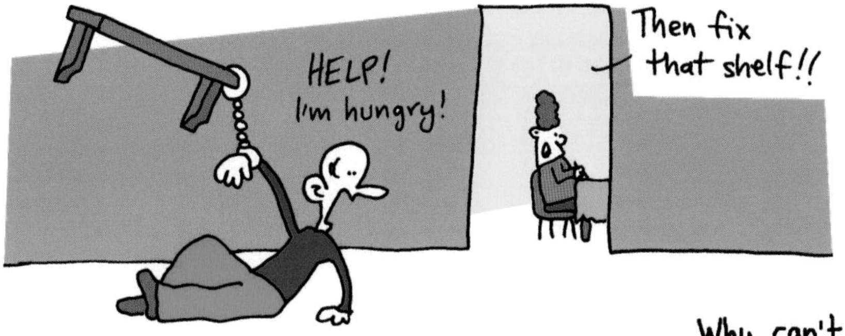
HELP!
I'm hungry!
Then fix that shelf!!

Or, why not use the handcuffs as trendy collars for Siamese Dachshunds.

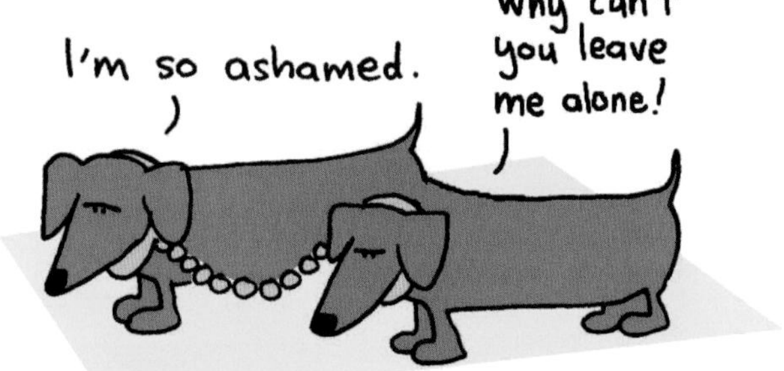
I'm so ashamed.
Why can't you leave me alone!

LUBRICANT!

Marvellous, adaptable stuff this. Use to banish annoying squeaks (doors, mice, granny's new artificial hip), or create slippy 'ice rinks' for pet hamsters, or as a cheap alternative to costly olive oil, or as Kylie-esque lip and cheek gloss, or as fake slug trails to annoy garden-proud neighbours, or guarantee yourself some space on public transport by using it as trick snot.

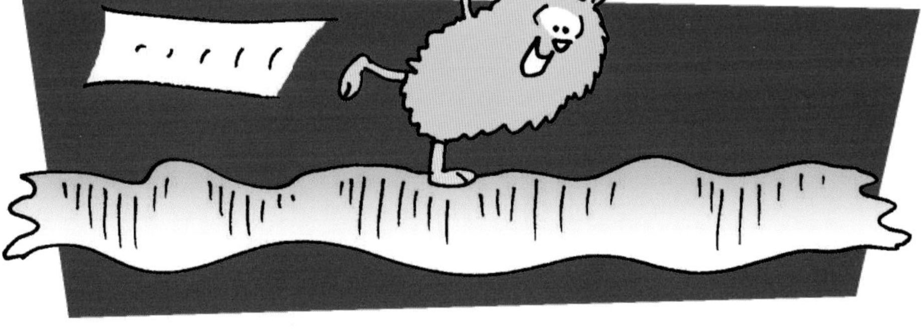
WEEEEE!

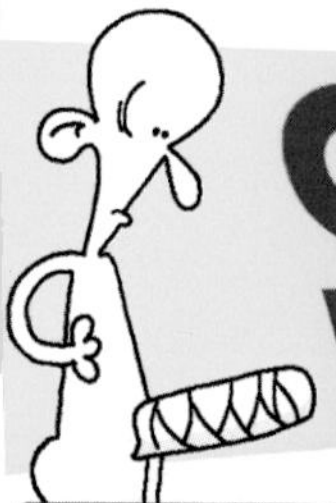

SEX SAFETY TIPS

Make love, not a trip to Casualty!

NEVER HUG TOO HARD WEARING BABY OIL!

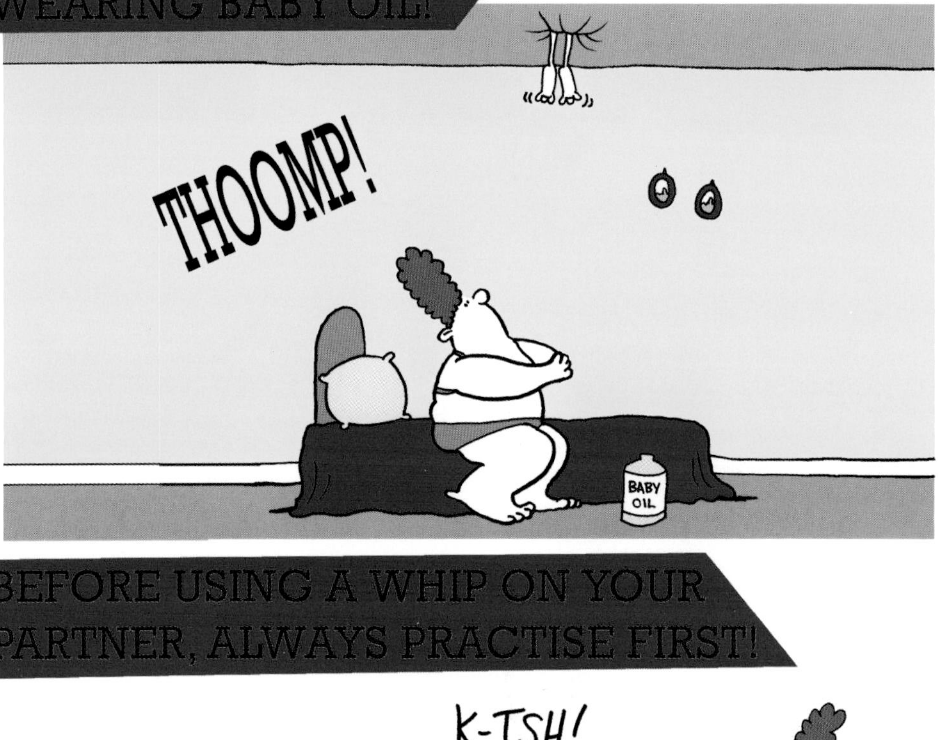
THOOMP!
BABY OIL

BEFORE USING A WHIP ON YOUR PARTNER, ALWAYS PRACTISE FIRST!

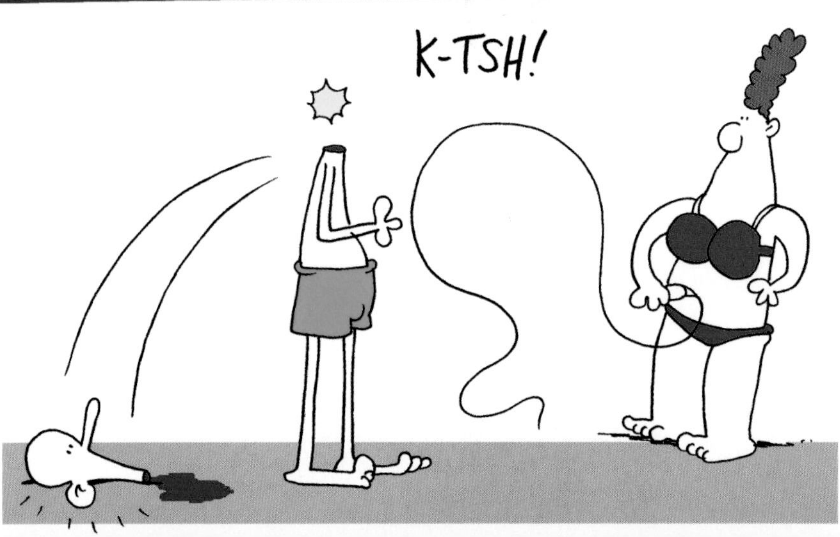
K-TSH!

AVOID SEX OUTDOORS IN THE WINTER!

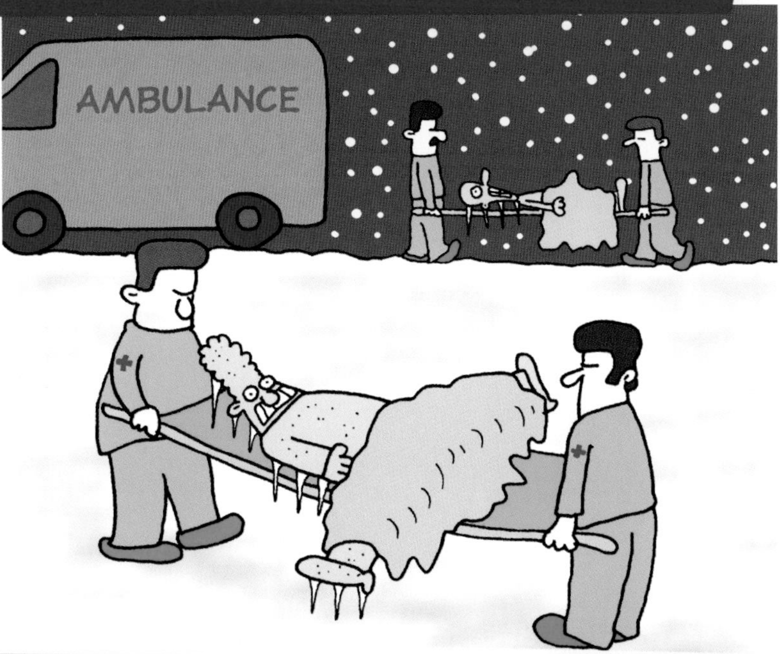
AMBULANCE

DURING SEXY DANCES, BE CAREFUL SUSPENDERS DO NOT SNAP

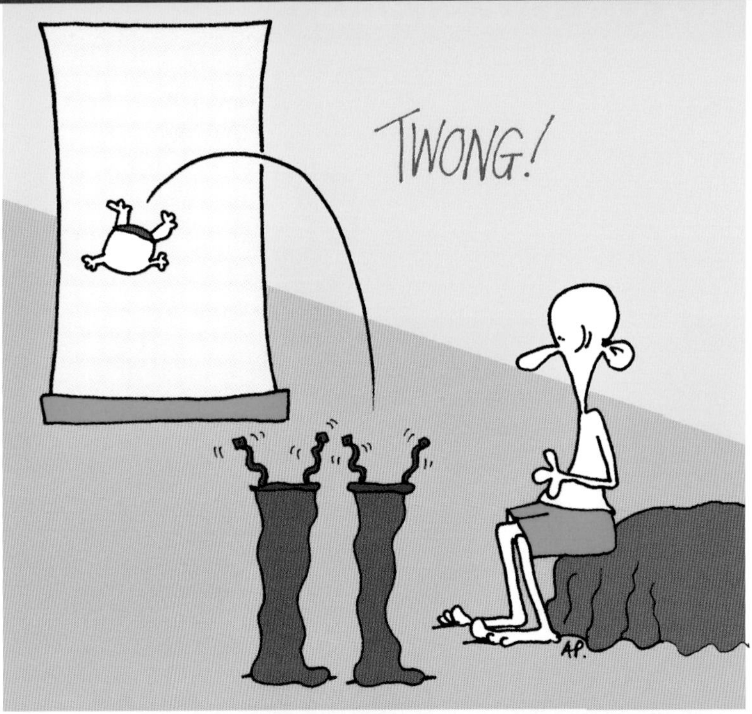
TWONG!
AP.

BOOBS SHOULD NOT BE ALLOWED TO BOUNCE AROUND TOO MUCH DURING SEX!

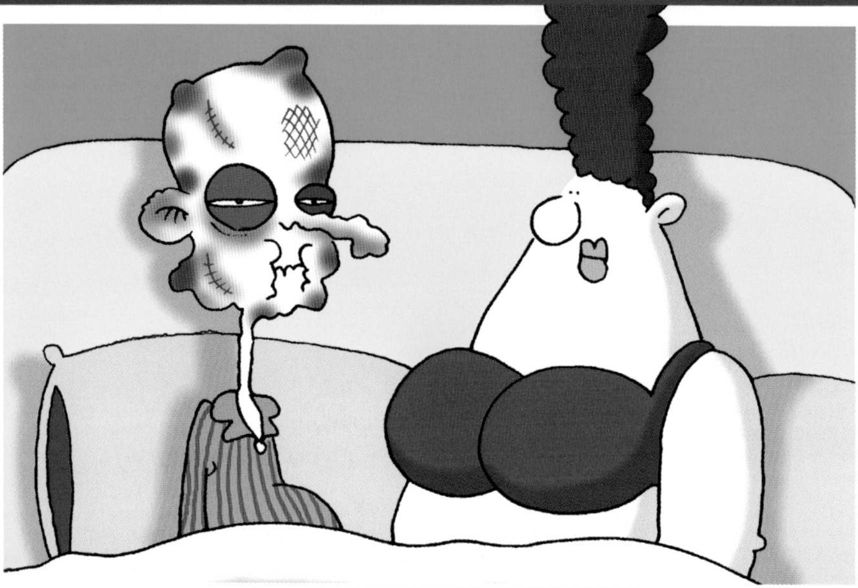

IT'S NEVER A GOOD IDEA TO HAVE SEX ON THE STAIRS!

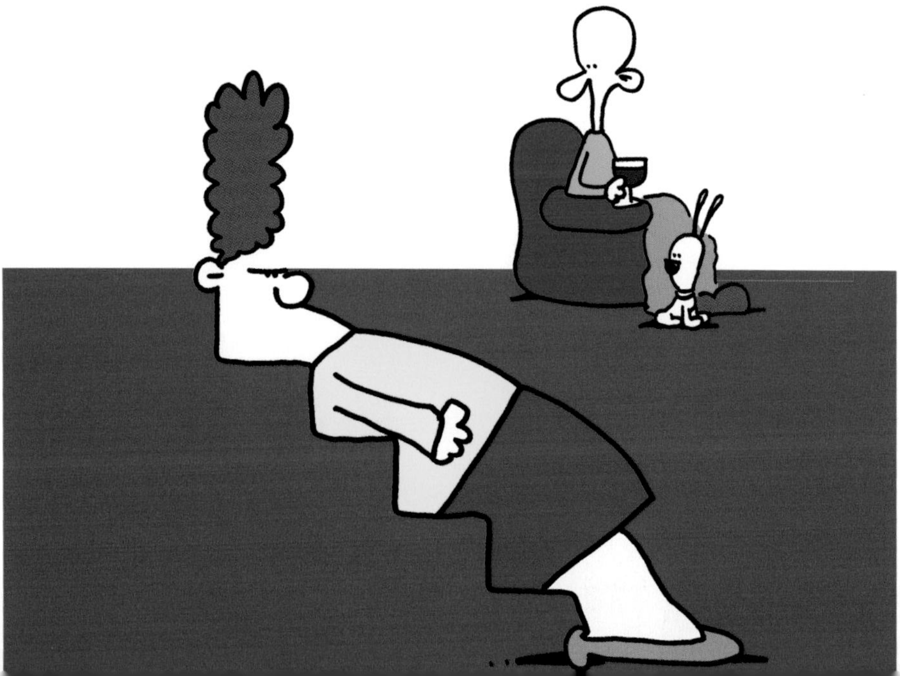

BE CAREFUL WHEN HAVING SEX IN YOUR BACK GARDEN!

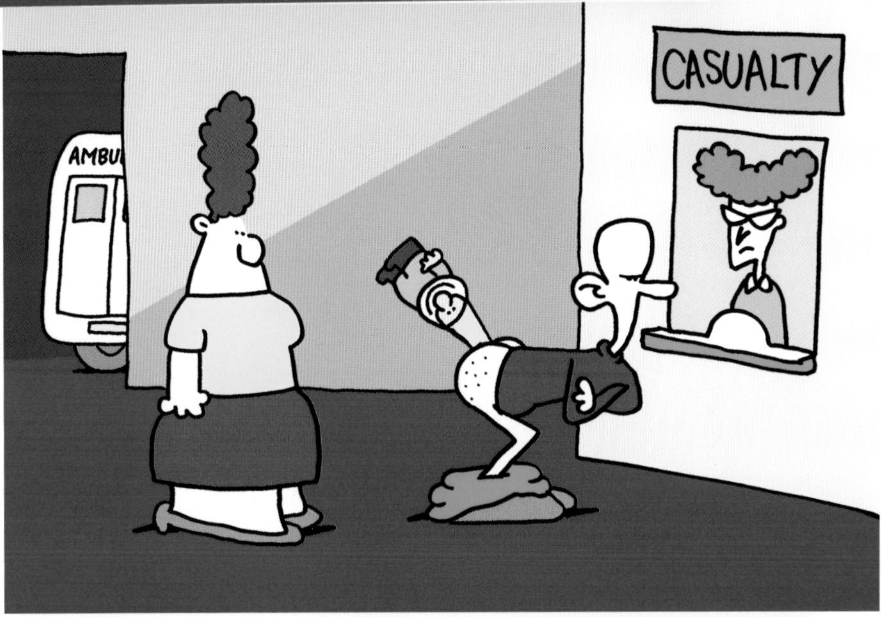

AMBU
CASUALTY

NEVER GO FOR A PEE IMMEDIATELY AFTER HAVING SEX!

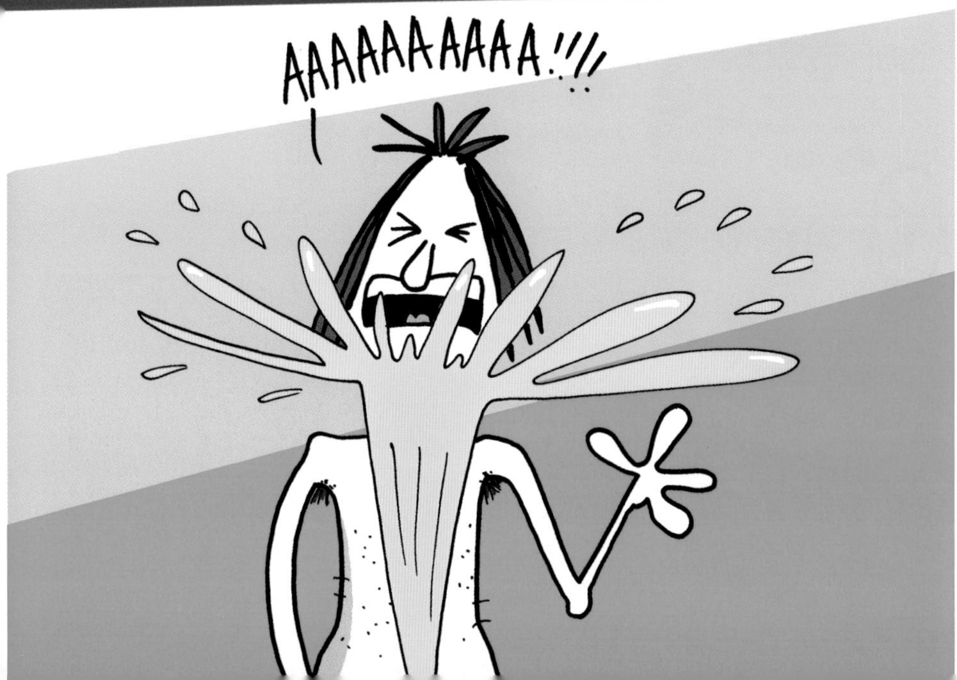

AAAAAAAAAA!!!

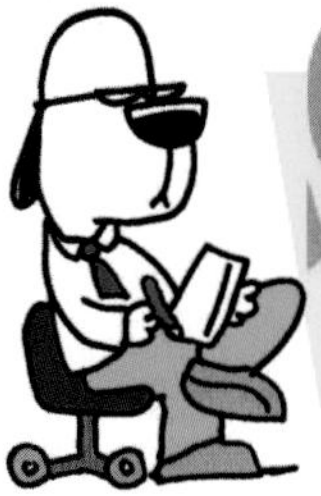

SEX MYTHS with Dr. Dog

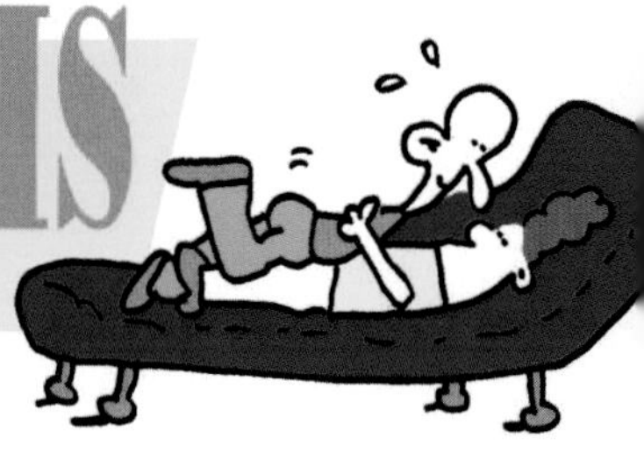

After farting in bed, sex is the second biggest cause of relationship break-downs – narrowl beating skid marks down the side of the toilet (3rd place!?!). You can't talk to each other abou your sex dilemmas in case it works and you stay together, so talk to Dr. Dog. He can't talk eithe But he can write rubbish down...

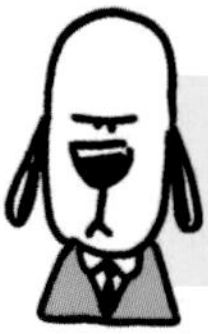

MYTH: You can't get pregnant the first time you have sex?

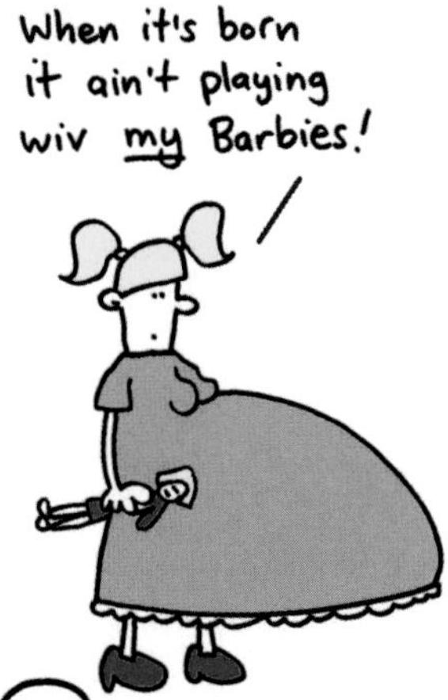
When it's born it ain't playing wiv my Barbies!

Doctor Doggie says: 100% true. The randy, excited, spotty teenage male will have come long before he enters (Approximately when he touches his zipper). HOWEVER if you're working-class (with dodgy dyed hair, sunbed orange, lots of H Samuel jewellery, rolls of flab you flaunt over your too-tight jeans, and have no prospects whatsoever) you WILL most certainly get pregnant the first time. This is a convenient reminder that you've actually done it - you'll have been too wasted to actually remember!...

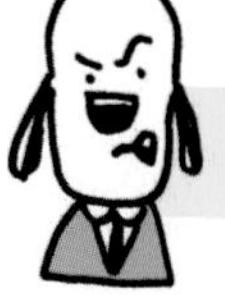

MYTH: You can't get pregnant standing up?

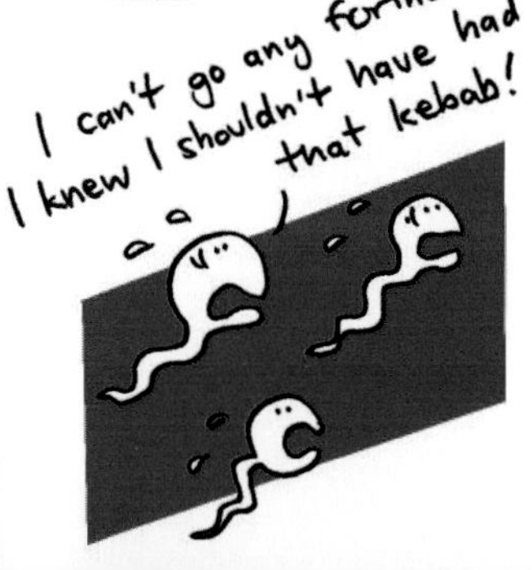
I can't go any further!
I knew I shouldn't have had that kebab!

Doctor Doggie says: True. Although, if you actually managed to succeed having sex standing up, you deserve a knighthood, never mind a baby. But, scientifically-speaking, sperm are just like men. Lazy. They can't be arsed with all that swimming upstream. Besides, it's much more fun running down a leg – it's just like a slide. Wee-heee.

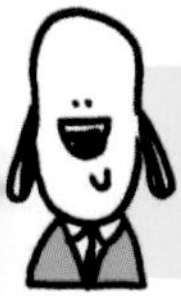

MYTH: If you have sex in the bath, the pumping action creates a vacuum and you get stuck?

Doctor Doggie says: Of course this is TRUE. Worse than being rescued by firemen, is the fact that you'll probably be stuck facing each other. And, there's the added peril of who gets the tap end. But, hey at least this'll be the only time you experience a really good suck.

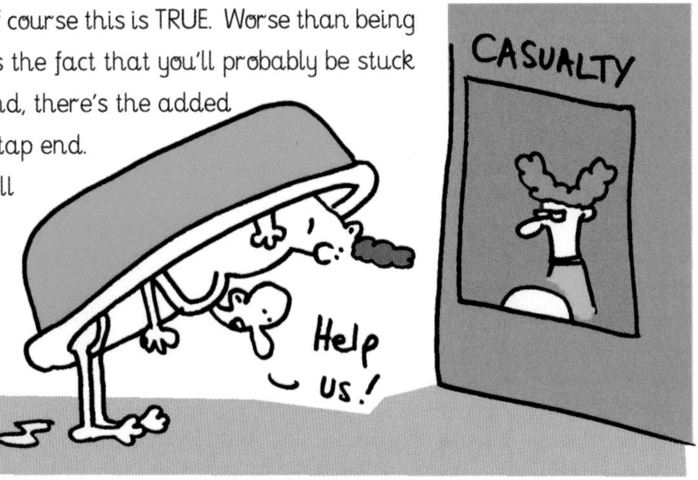
CASUALTY
Help us!

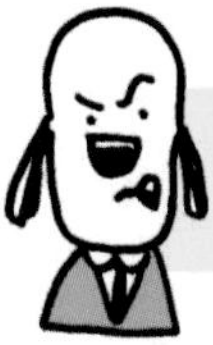

MYTH: You can get pregnant if you swallow sperm?

Doctor Doggie says: Semi-true. Swallowing sperm actually results in the fertilisation of your tonsils - your larynx will be home to the developing tonsetus for 15 days before hatching into lots of adorable baby tonsils. You may opt to become a surrogate mum to thousands of modern kids who've had their own tonsils ripped from them at the very mention of a sore throat. HANG ON! What are you doing even thinking about swallowing sperm?? Does he voluntarily do any housework?!? Furthermore, sperm is 13.7 calories per gulp. That's a whole lick of a biscuit!

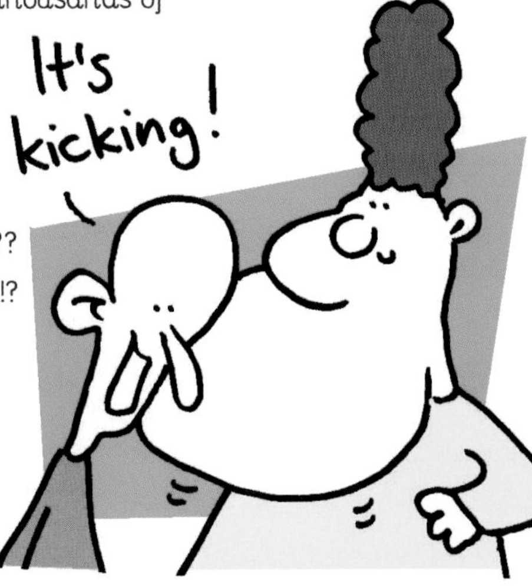
It's kicking!

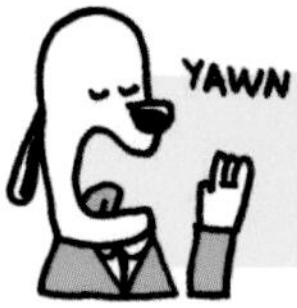
YAWN

MYTH: If your boyfriend wants anal it means he's gay?

Doctor Doggie says: If you're that naive, no wonder he wants to be a gay. However, there's a 1 in 473 chance that the real reason could just simply be that your vagina is just way too slack after all that sleeping around, and only your botty-hole provides a tight enough circumference!

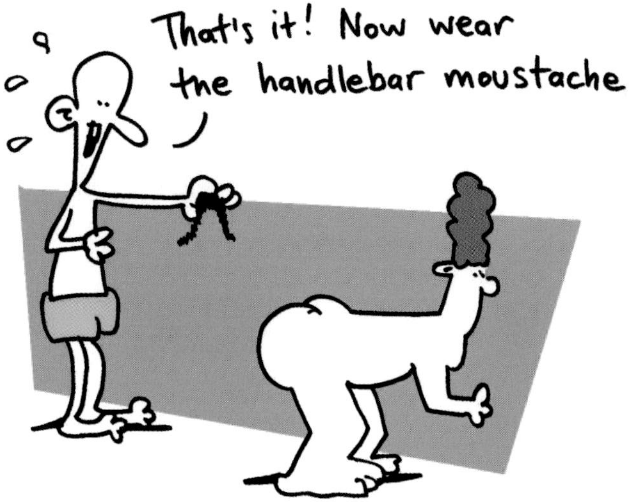
That's it! Now wear the handlebar moustache

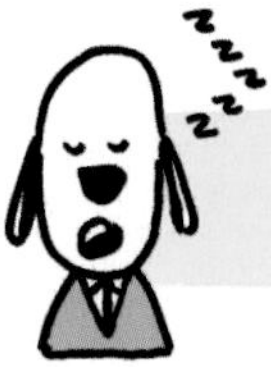
zzzz

MYTH: If you masturbate you'll go blind!

Doctor Doggie says: Of course. What happens is you experience such sublime pleasure that all your blood vessels burst, and voila, you go blind. On the plus side, your blind stick is a great chick/hunk magnet, you'll never have to see how ugly your one-night stand is, and Braille books are very arousing when rubbed over the skin!

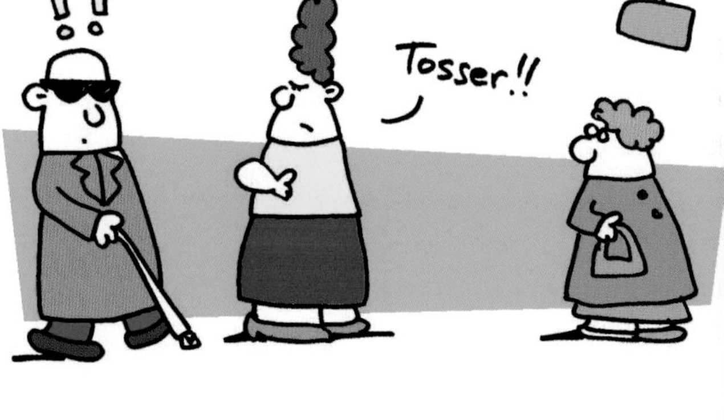
!?
Tosser!!

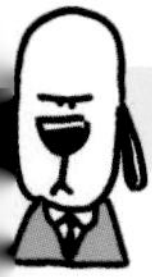

MYTH: All men suffer impotence at some time?

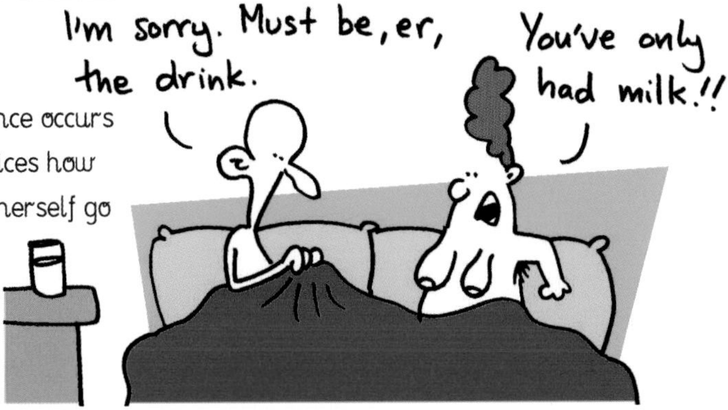
I'm sorry. Must be, er, the drink.
You've only had milk!!

Doctor Doggie says:
Of course. Divvy. Impotence occurs when the man finally notices how much the woman has let herself go (approx. 3 months into a relationship, or 2 weeks after the wedding, if you're lucky).

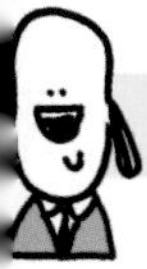

MYTH: Penis size doesn't matter?

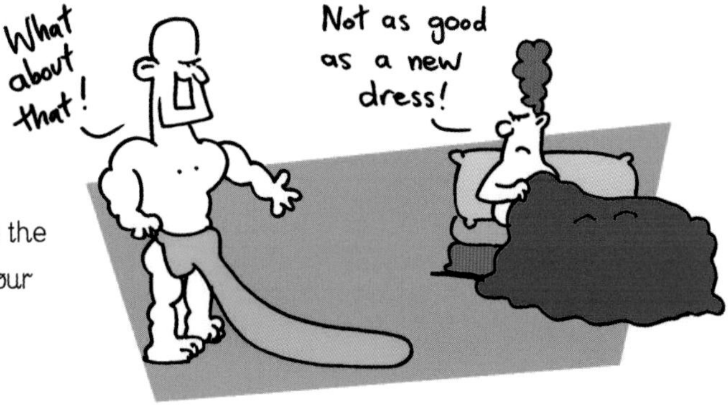
What about that!
Not as good as a new dress!

Doctor Doggie says:
Penis prowess is irrelevant. She'll never climax whatever your size. The only thing that counts to the selfish trollop is the size of your wallet. So ignore her and please yourself.

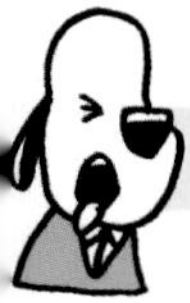

MYTH: The older you get, the lower your libido?

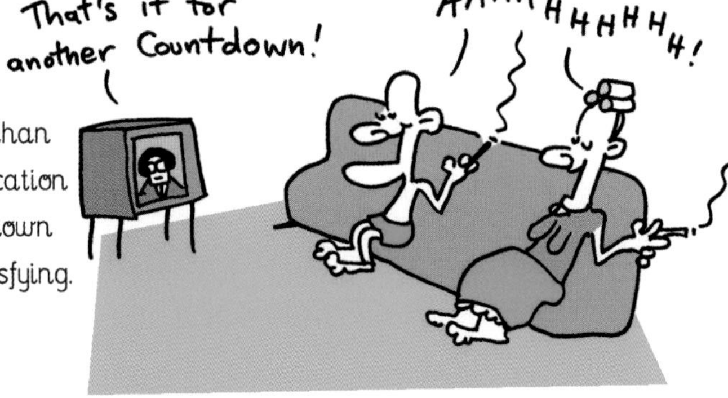
That's it for another Countdown!
AAAAHHHHHHH!

Doctor Doggie says:
Naturally. Boobies by the knees, piles that are longer than the willy, and the only lubrication is dribble!?! Anyway Countdown is far more exciting and satisfying. Mmmm, Carol...

HOW TO MAKE YOUR OWN
Porn Movie!

Costumes

MEN, WEAR THE FOLLOWING:
- HANDLEBAR MOUSTACHE
- BOILER SUIT
- CHEESY GRIN

WOMEN: WEAR AS LITTLE
AS POSSIBLE, PREFERABLY
RED AND SEE-THROUGH:
- STOCKINGS & SUSSIES
- NIPPLE TASSELS
- A THONG 4 SIZES TOO
  SMALL

NOTE: YOU MUST SHAVE
ALL HAIRY ZONES,
ESPECIALLY THE OFTEN
MISSED HAIRY BUM HOLE!
(USE HIS RAZOR OF COURSE!)

Music

PLAY AWFUL, EASY-LISTENING JAZZ MUSIC IN THE BACKGROUND.

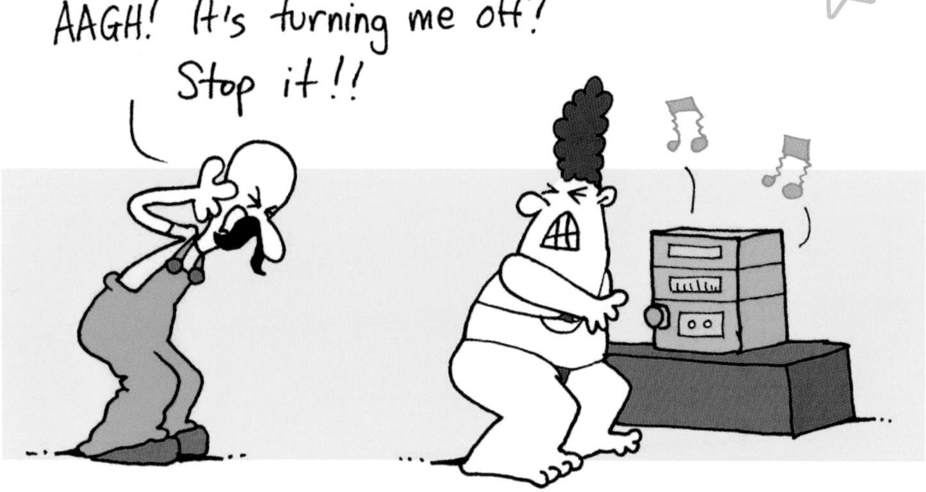
AAGH! It's turning me off! Stop it!!

Accessories

HAVE A SELECTION OF SEXY TOYS TO HAND.

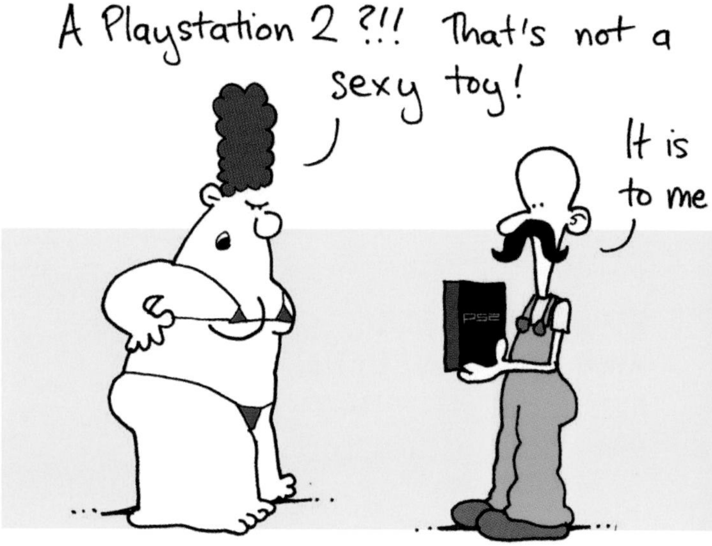
A Playstation 2 ?!! That's not a sexy toy!
It is to me
PS2

Script USE THE FOLLOWING SAMPLE SCRIPT AS A GUIDE:

Scene One - Front Door - Day

<DOORBELL RINGS>

HER: Oh, HELLO there, handsome!! I'm all alone, you know!

HIM: Hello Madam. I'm here to fiddle with your pipes.

HER: Ooooh yes, big boy! They're dripping wet. I think you need to stuff something up them.

HIM: Don't worry, I'll give them a good going over. Why don't I pull out my big tool and get to work.

HER: OOOOOOOOhhhh! Tee hee hee!!!

<BONKING BEGINS>

Action!!!

BONK YOUR ARSE AWAY UNTIL EVERYTHING FEELS SLIGHTLY RAW (OR YOU GET BORED)

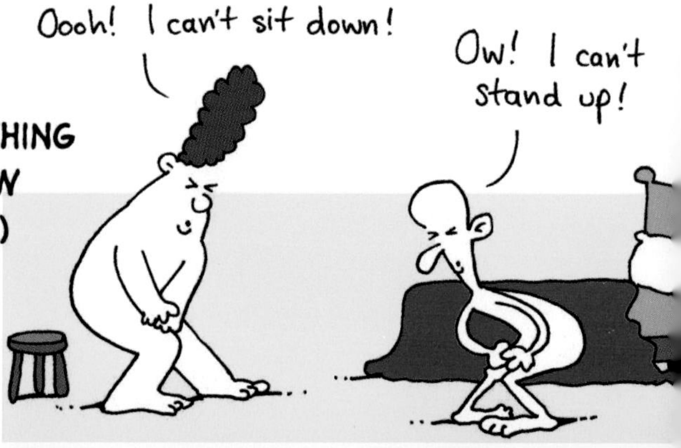
Oooh! I can't sit down!
Ow! I can't stand up!

THE "HOW GOOD AT SEX ARE YOU?" QUIZ

The only people who are naturally good at sex are prostitutes, priests and librarians. Don't bother asking your copulator how you rate 'cos they'll only lie - either to spite you or protect you, and besides, who cares what they think. Just take this penetrating quiz…

1. At what age did you lose your virginity?

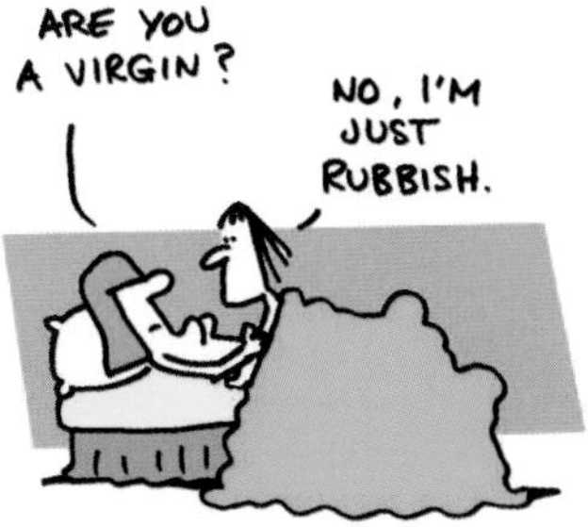
ARE YOU A VIRGIN?
NO, I'M JUST RUBBISH.

a) 8-11
b) 12-14 (you're a late developer)
c) 15-22 (a Christian)
d) 23-freak

2. How many sexual partners have you had?

a) 4, plus one hand
b) 5-98 ½ (your mum came in)
c) 99-109 (101-108 you wish to forget due to beer goggles)
d) 148-246 (you're a footballer or a liar)

3. What's your favourite position?

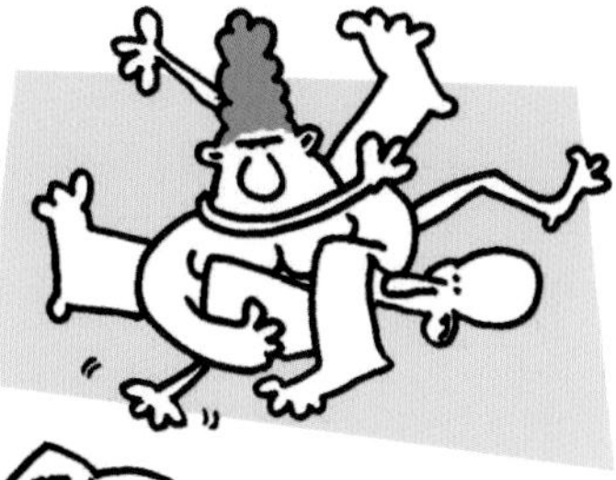

a) With someone else
b) The quickie
c) Kama Sutra No.7255
d) Orgy

4. What do you think of oral sex?

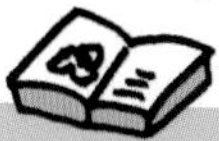

a) I don't like talking dirty
b) Fine, if "IT" is covered in gallons of cream, chocolate sauce, booze, chips, ice-cream, strawberries and sweets
c) Do you mind, I've just eaten
d) Mmm, feeling a bit peckish now

5. What's the most number of times a night you've done it?

a) ½ - Mum interrupted, again, Freudian pervert
b) 13 (but you were on your own)
c) 22 - not with the same person though
d) Once, but the bout lasted 3 days

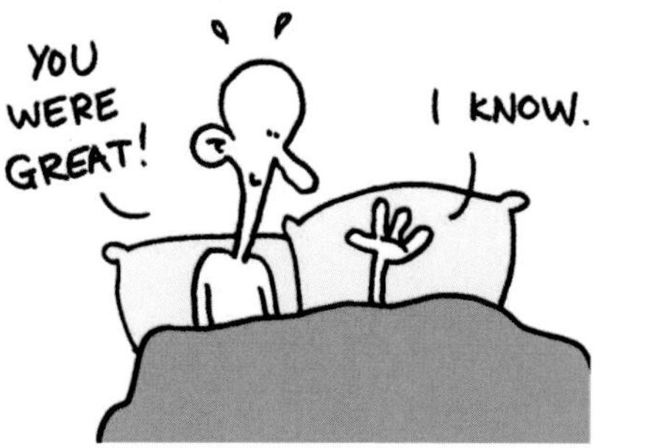
YOU WERE GREAT!
I KNOW.

6. It's your wedding night, and naturally you're rat-arsed, do you:

a) Fall unconscious on the nuptial bed ... start as you mean to go on
b) Give the performance of a lifetime to the love of your life (or so they'll think – they're unconscious)
c) Have a 2 minute stab at it and then give up, you're knackered
d) What!! You've already done it twice with the bridesmaids/vicar

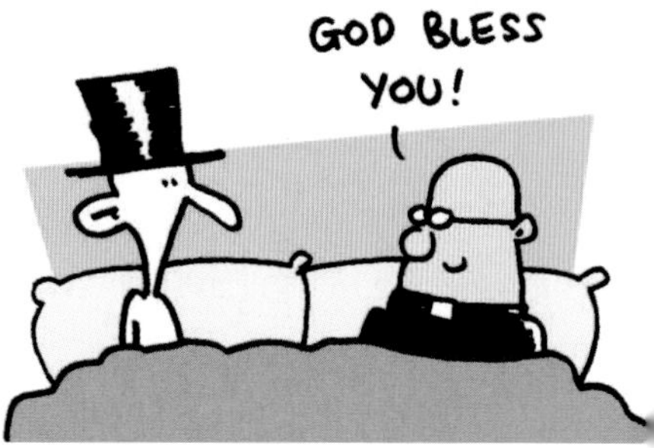
GOD BLESS YOU!

7. You catch your parents at it, do you:

a) Spontaneously drop down dead
b) Home movie them for future blackmailing
c) Home movie them so they can critique their performance later
d) Home movie them – there's money to be made on the internet

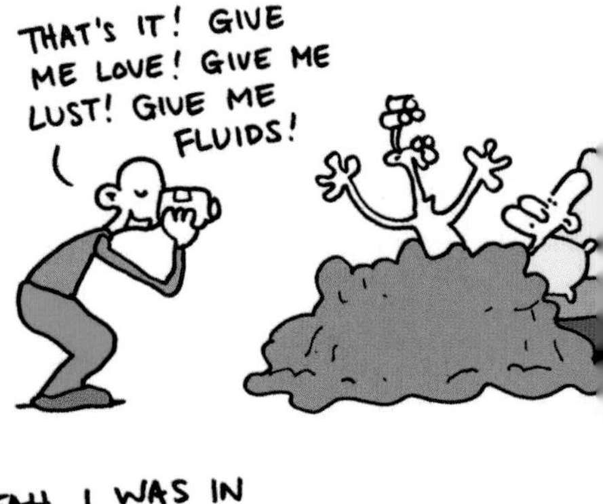
THAT'S IT! GIVE ME LOVE! GIVE ME LUST! GIVE ME FLUIDS!

8. On a one-night stand, do you pretend you are:

a) A porn star
b) A fireman or firewoman (men can show off their hose action)
c) An ER doctor
d) All of the above. Who cares? You'll never see them again

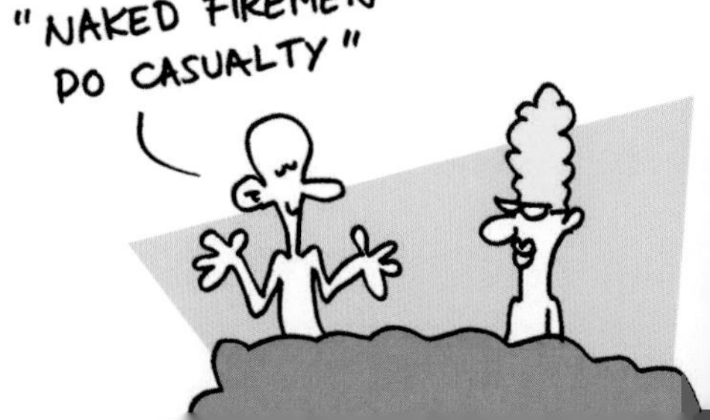
YEAH, I WAS IN "NAKED FIREMEN DO CASUALTY"

9. Your partner wants to do it up the bum, do you:

a) Cry and tell their mum
b) Take the butt plug out first
c) Agree, well, you've been constipated for ages
d) Just the bum? There's plenty more orifices going

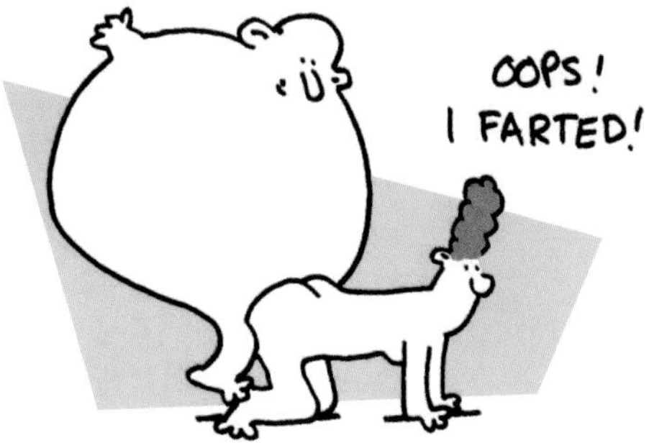
OOPS!
I FARTED!

10. How long, on average, do you spend on foreplay?
a) Ages, you love them, about 3 minutes
b) Longer than they deserve, about 3 minutes
c) Too long, about 3 minutes
d) The national average, about 3 minutes

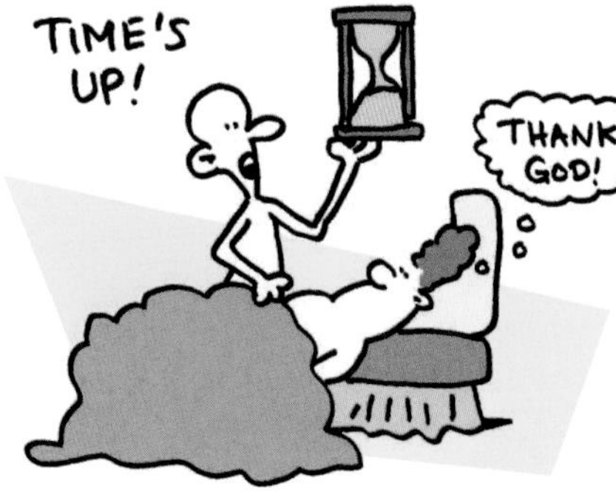
TIME'S UP!
THANK GOD!

11. Your partner wants to introduce porn into your sex life, do you:

a) Say "About time. Bring it on"
b) Quickly secretly check she hasn't found your hidden stash
c) Quickly secretly check he hasn't found your hidden stash
d) Scream when you realise the Reader's Wife is your mum

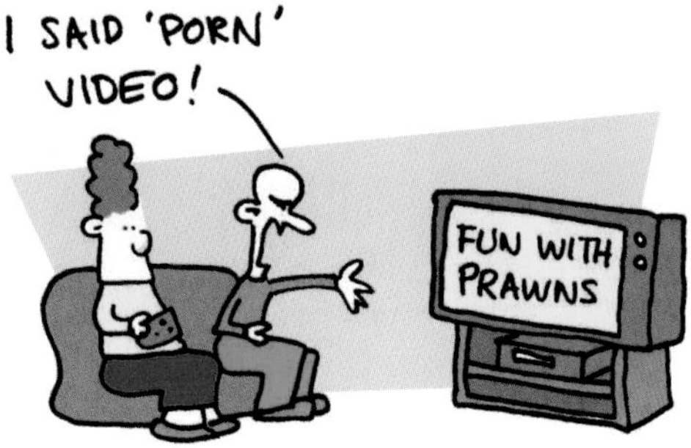
I SAID 'PORN' VIDEO!
FUN WITH PRAWNS

12. You suspect your partner's not enjoying the session, what do you do?

a) Stuff 'em
b) Stuff 'em
c) Stuff 'em
d) Stuff 'em

RESULTS If you picked mostly:
a) You think you're crap in bed and you're right
b) You think you're average in bed but you're crap
c) You think you're great in bed but you're crap
d) You think you're amazing in bed but you're really crap

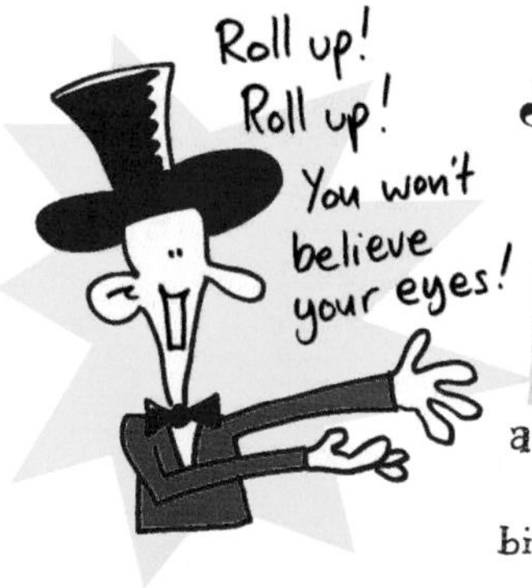

Roll up! Roll up! You won't believe your eyes!

The Incredible Sex Freak Show

Forget bearded ladies, 6-legged weirdos and strangely alluring hunchbacks. These are the NEW freaks of the 21st Century Freak Show, featurin bizarre individuals who not only have sex, but good se

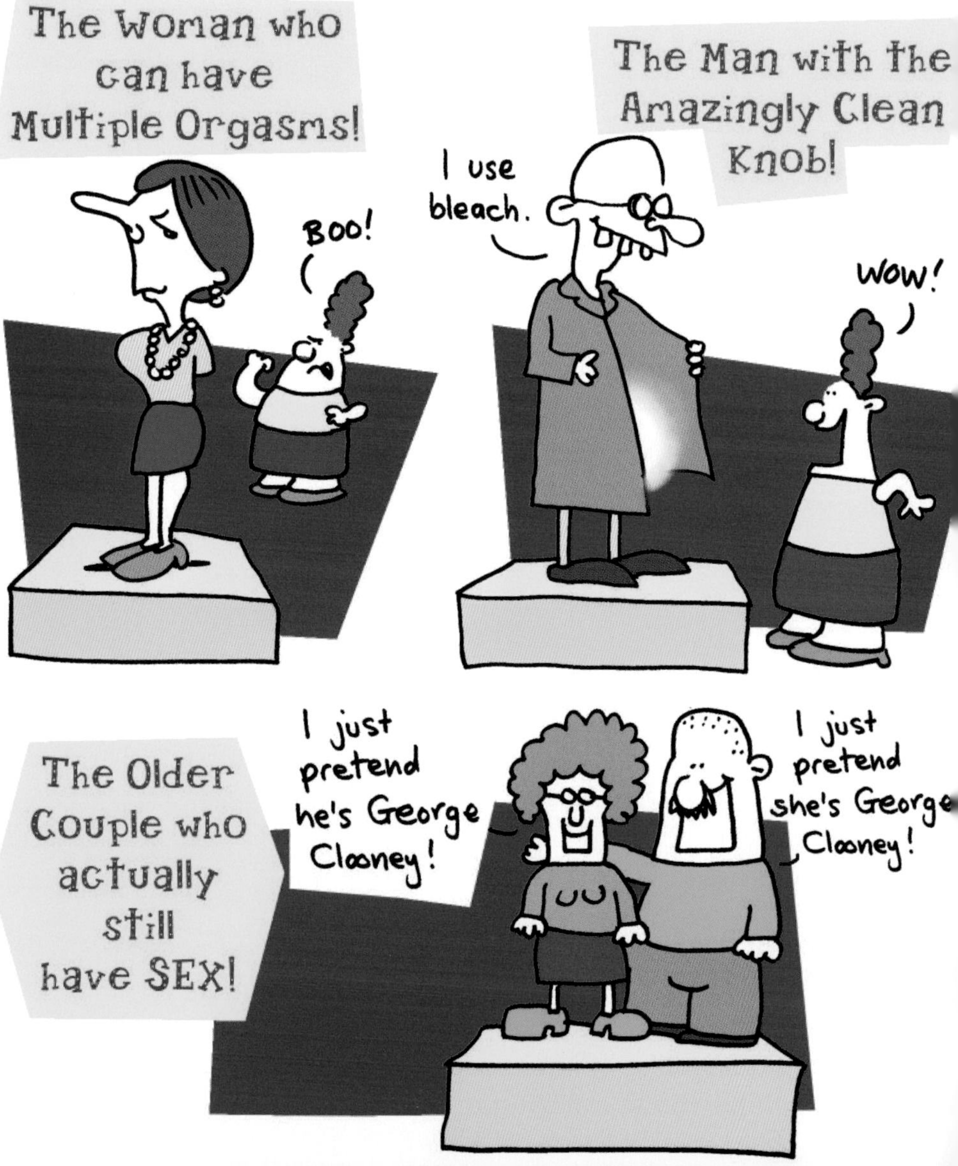

The Woman who can have Multiple Orgasms!
BOO!
The Man with the Amazingly Clean Knob!
I use bleach.
WOW!
The Older Couple who actually still have SEX!
I just pretend he's George Clooney!
I just pretend she's George Clooney!

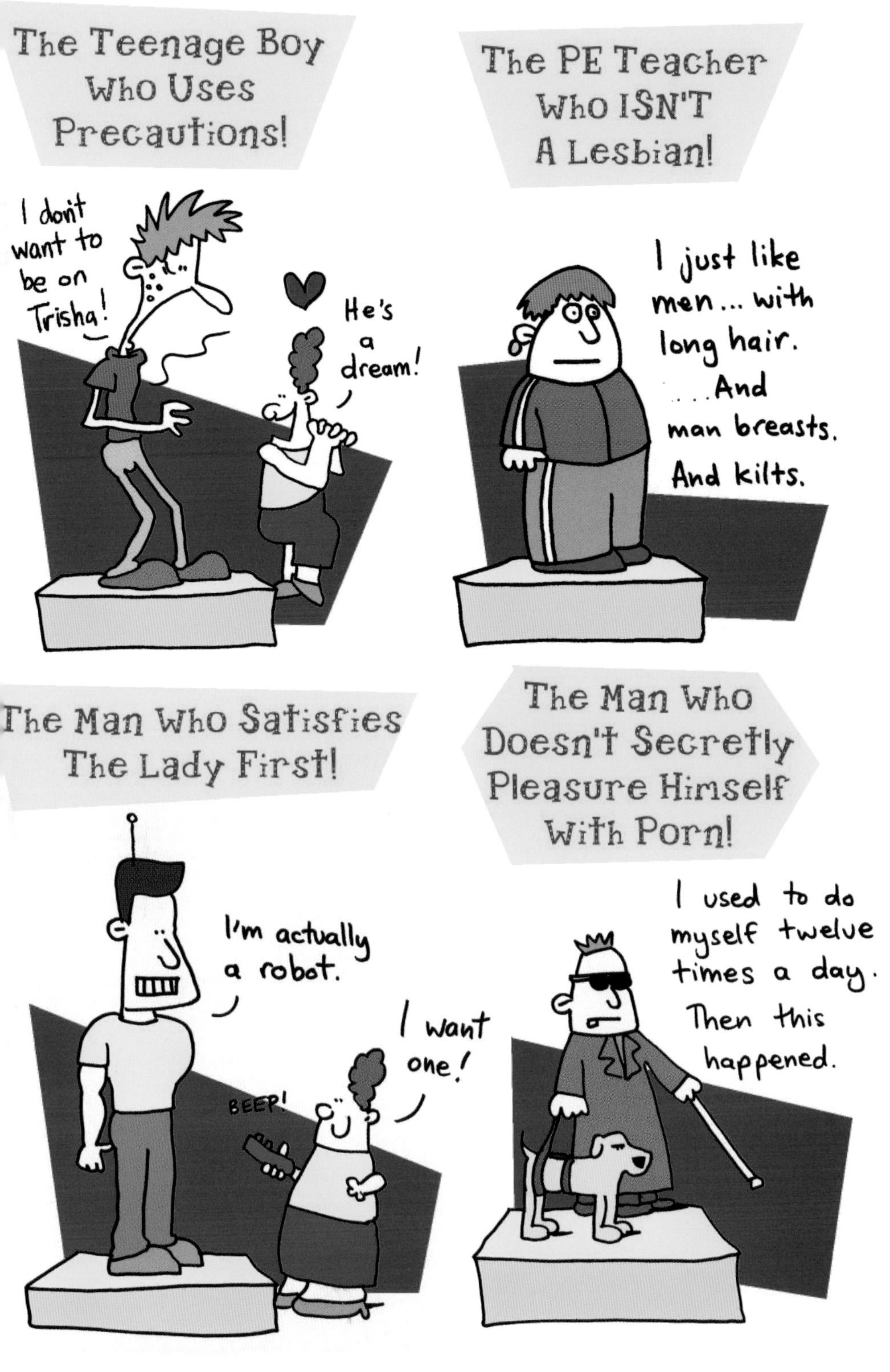
The Teenage Boy Who Uses Precautions!
I don't want to be on Trisha!
He's a dream!
The PE Teacher Who ISN'T A Lesbian!
I just like men... with long hair.
....And man breasts.
And kilts.
The Man Who Satisfies The Lady First!
I'm actually a robot.
BEEP!
I want one!
The Man Who Doesn't Secretly Pleasure Himself With Porn!
I used to do myself twelve times a day.
Then this happened.

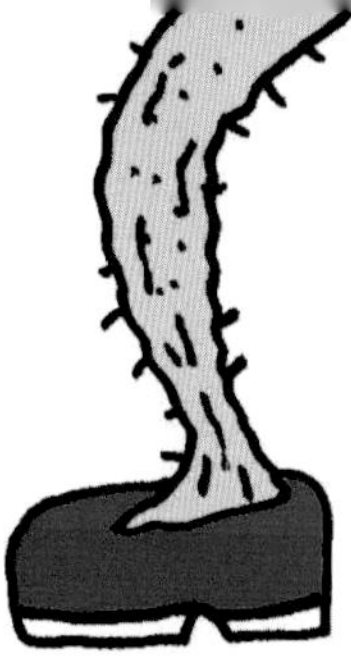

SEX for the ELDERLY!

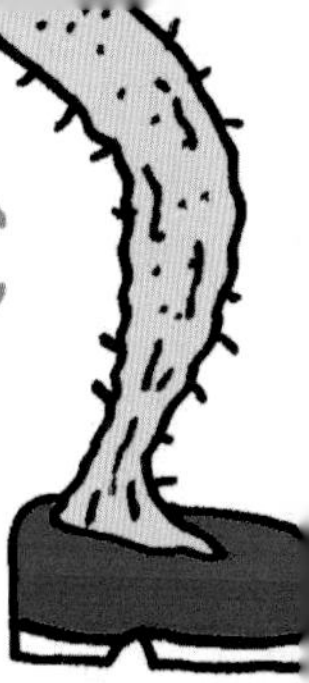

After you turn 27, sex becomes somewhat crap. The body becomes even more physically repulsive, the effort far outweighs the gain, and besides, 'Countdown' or 'Songs of Praise' is on the telly. You will now require mental, physical and neighbourly assistance to achieve any degree of sexual satisfaction…

1. Set a reasonable time limit (eg. 39 seconds) – if neither of you climax before the alarm goes off, so what, it's not as if you'll divorce, you're too decrepit. If, by some miracle, one of you does enjoy it, the loser has to pre-soften the hard toffees by sucking them.

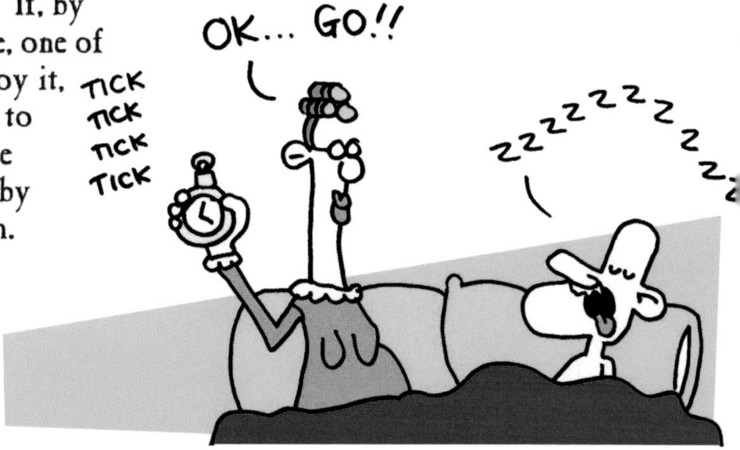
OK… GO!!
TICK
TICK
TICK
TICK
ZZZZZZZZZZZZ

2. Drink 14 gallons of gin (for females) or 27 litres of whiskey (if male) for much-needed spirit goggles. Only then can you forget how hideous they (and you) have become.

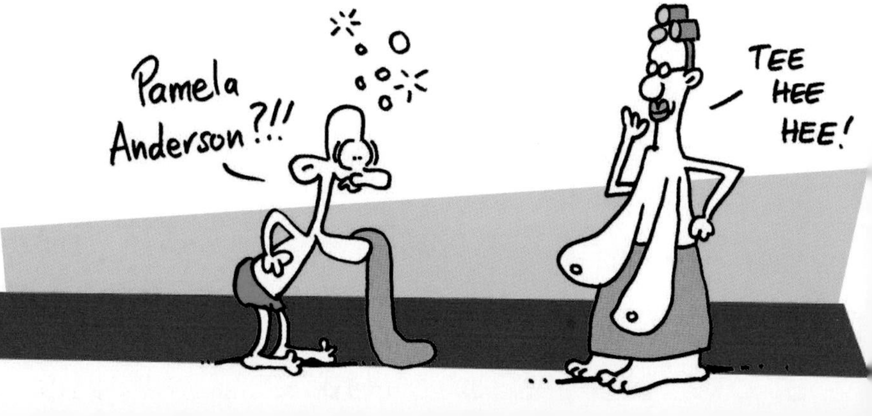
Pamela Anderson?!!
TEE HEE HEE!

3. Substitute boring, exhausting pointless foreplay for sexy video porn!

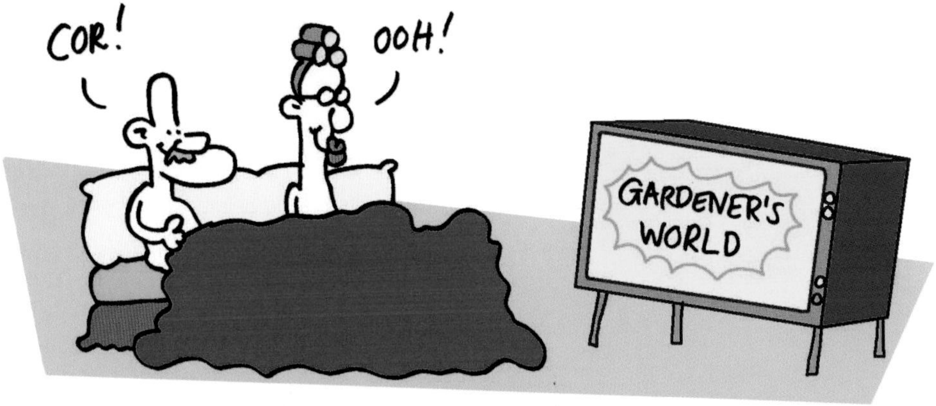
COR!
OOH!
GARDENER'S WORLD

4. Have defibrillators handy – your partner's screams may not necessarily mean they are having an orgasm.

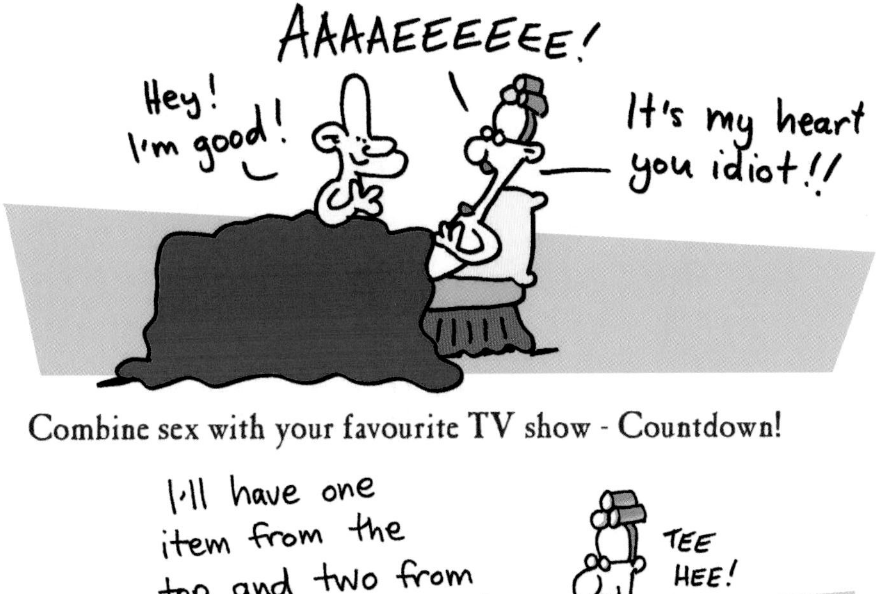
Hey! I'm good!
AAAAEEEEEEE!
It's my heart you idiot!!

5. Combine sex with your favourite TV show - Countdown!

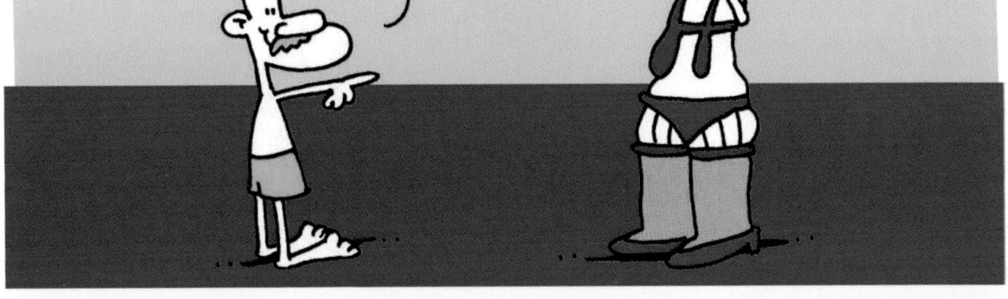
I'll have one item from the top and two from the bottom!
TEE HEE!

Sexual Positions for O.A.Ps

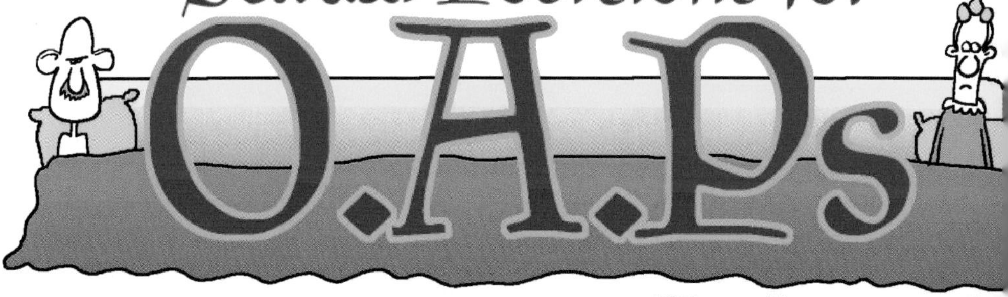

(Odorous Argumentative Pa

The ZIMMER position

An arthritis-friendly position, the real benefit being you don't have to smell their rancid cabbage stew breath. If your zimmer has been repossessed by meanie debt collectors in lieu of exorbitant council tax non-payment, or stolen by naughty but impressively imaginative joy-riders, then substitute with a supermarket trolley. If you feel guilty about permanently removing the trolley from the premises, just shag in the haemorrhoids treatment aisle – it's always deserted.

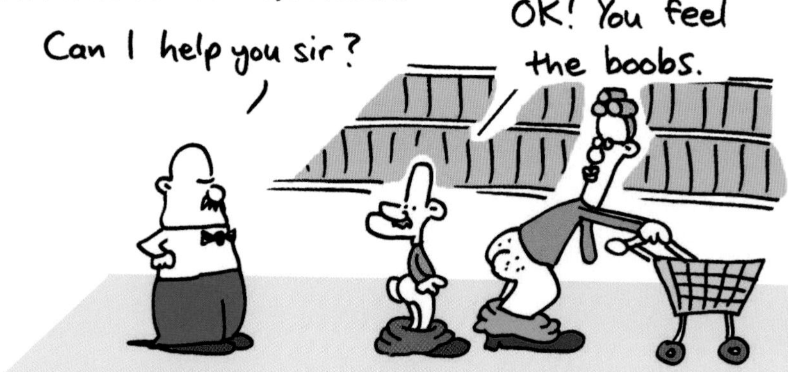
Can I help you sir?
OK! You feel the boobs.

The RECLINER position

Mocked by the young, but the recliner comes to us all. This greatest invention of the 20th Century allows the copulating couple to get easily back on their feet. Indeed, its reclining angles allow for deepest, darkest penetration.

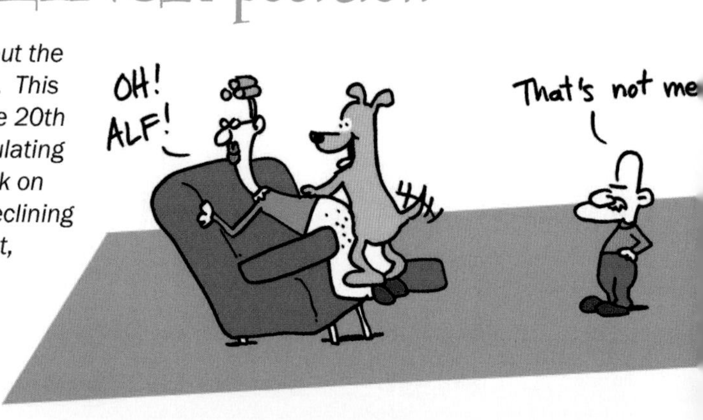
OH! ALF!
That's not me

The POST OFFICE position

Those pension-collecting queues at the post office before you get mugged take forever. Why not make old friends and pass the time by performing "The Doggie Conga". Just don't get confused about what hole you're posting your letters into.

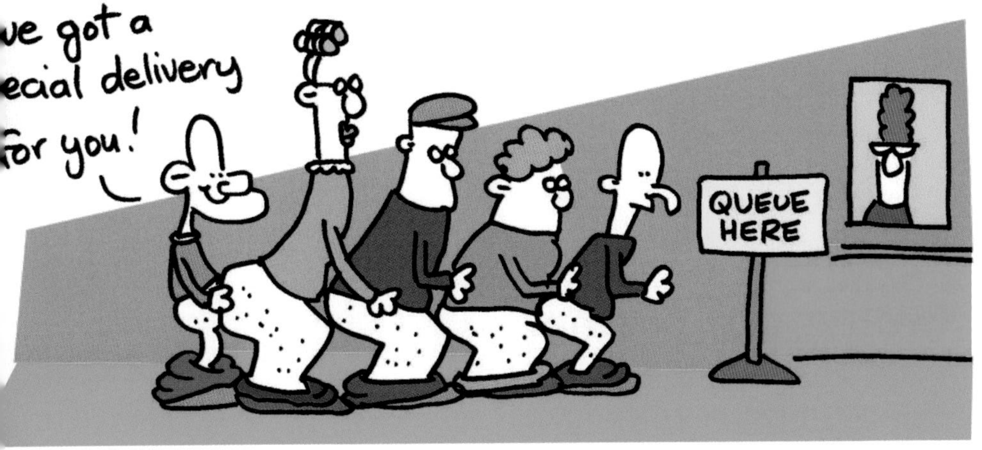

ve got a
ecial delivery
for you!
QUEUE HERE

The NATIONAL TRUST position

Ha, oldies don't actually like history, crumbly castles and droning guides, they go to stately homes for the myriad of secret shagging opportunities: hidden doors, heavy ceiling-high curtains, mazes, deserted rip-off cafes. Indeed, wrinklies always take packed lunches not because they're scraping by on benefits and can't afford the cafe, but because the boxes make great storage receptacles for cuffs and whips.

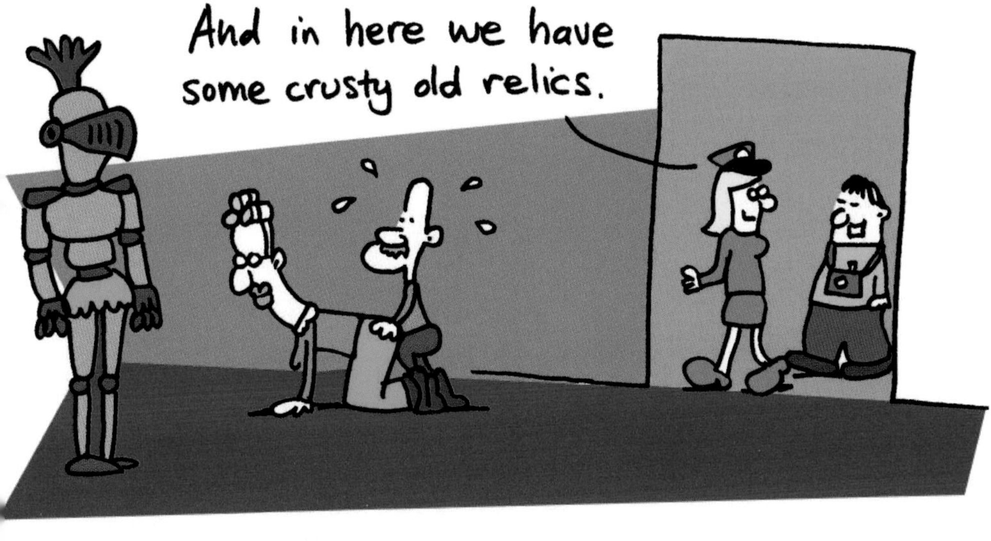

And in here we have some crusty old relics.

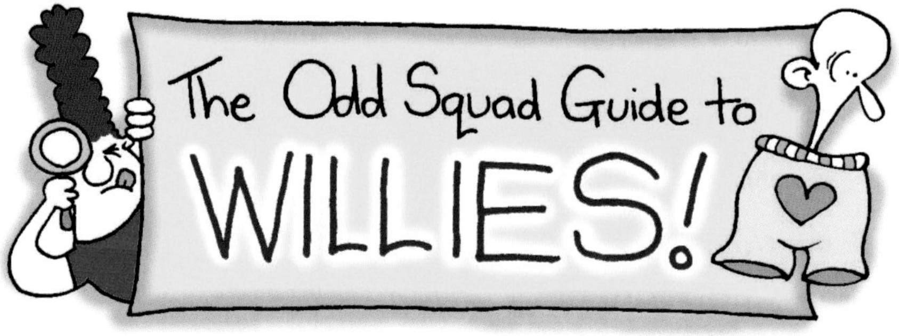
The Odd Squad Guide to
WILLIES!

THE TINKY WINKY!

SMALL, BUT CUTE. IF YOU'VE GOT ONE YOU BETTER HAVE A BRILLIANT PERSONALITY!

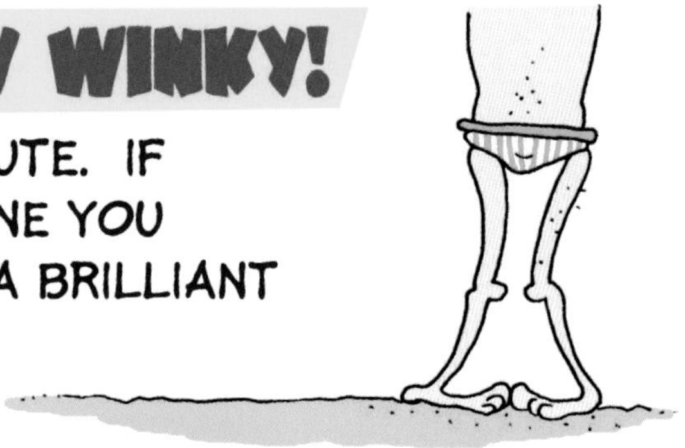

THE CHUB!

THE SAME SIZE AND SHAPE AS A POTATO CROQUETTE, BUT NOT AS TASTY.

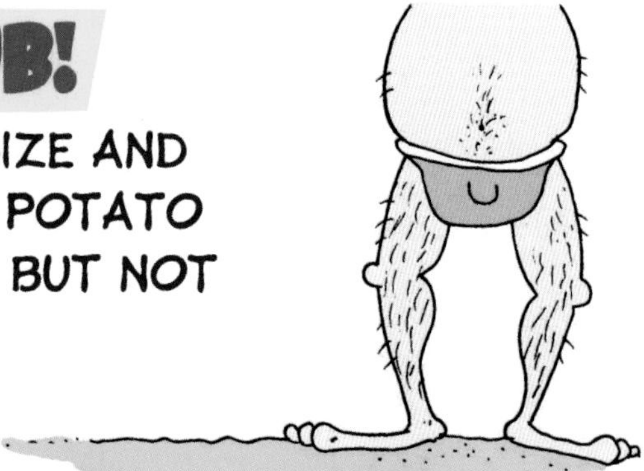

THE TREE STUMP!

WHAT IT LACKS IN LENGTH IT MAKES UP FOR IN WIDTH. IDEALLY NEEDS A GIRL THAT'S BEEN AROUND THE BLOCK A FEW TIMES.

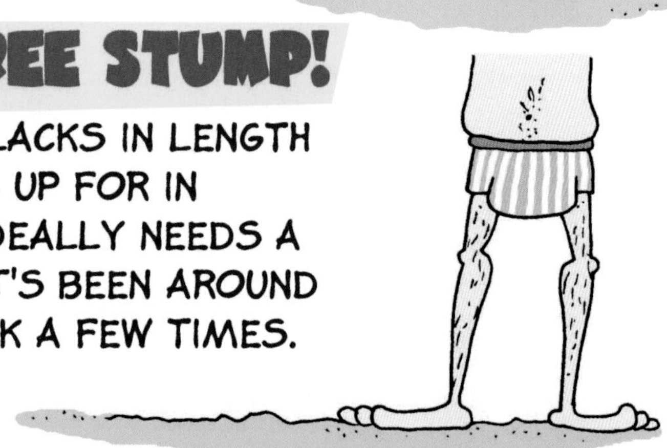

R. DONKEY!

SOFT, STRONG AND VERY LONG. CAN ALSO BE USED TO HAMMER IN NAILS AND CARRY SHOPPING HOME.

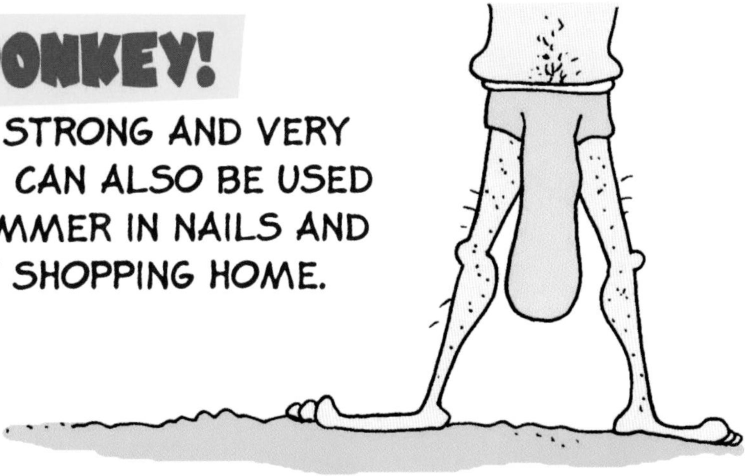

FIREHOSE SAM!

VERY RARE – ONLY ONE OR TWO IN EXISTENCE. A PROTECTED SPECIES MAINLY FOUND IN AFRICA.

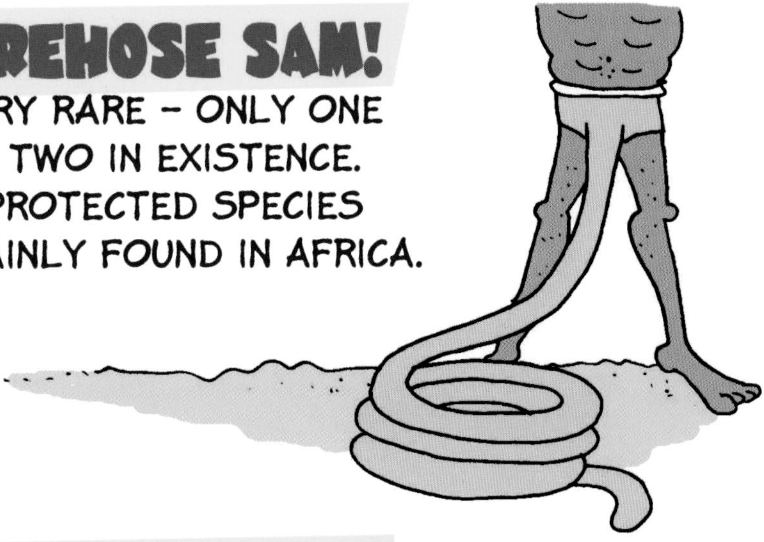

THE WRINKLED WINKLE!

AN O.A.P. (OLD AGED PENIS). NO LONGER SERVES ANY USEFUL PURPOSE, ALTHOUGH CAN BE USED AS A HANDY BOOKMARK.

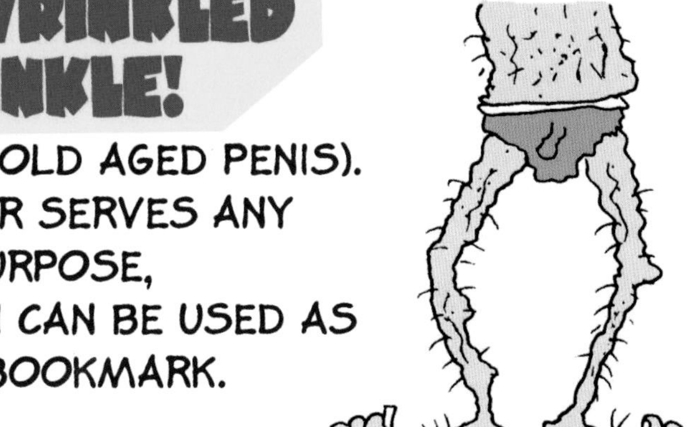

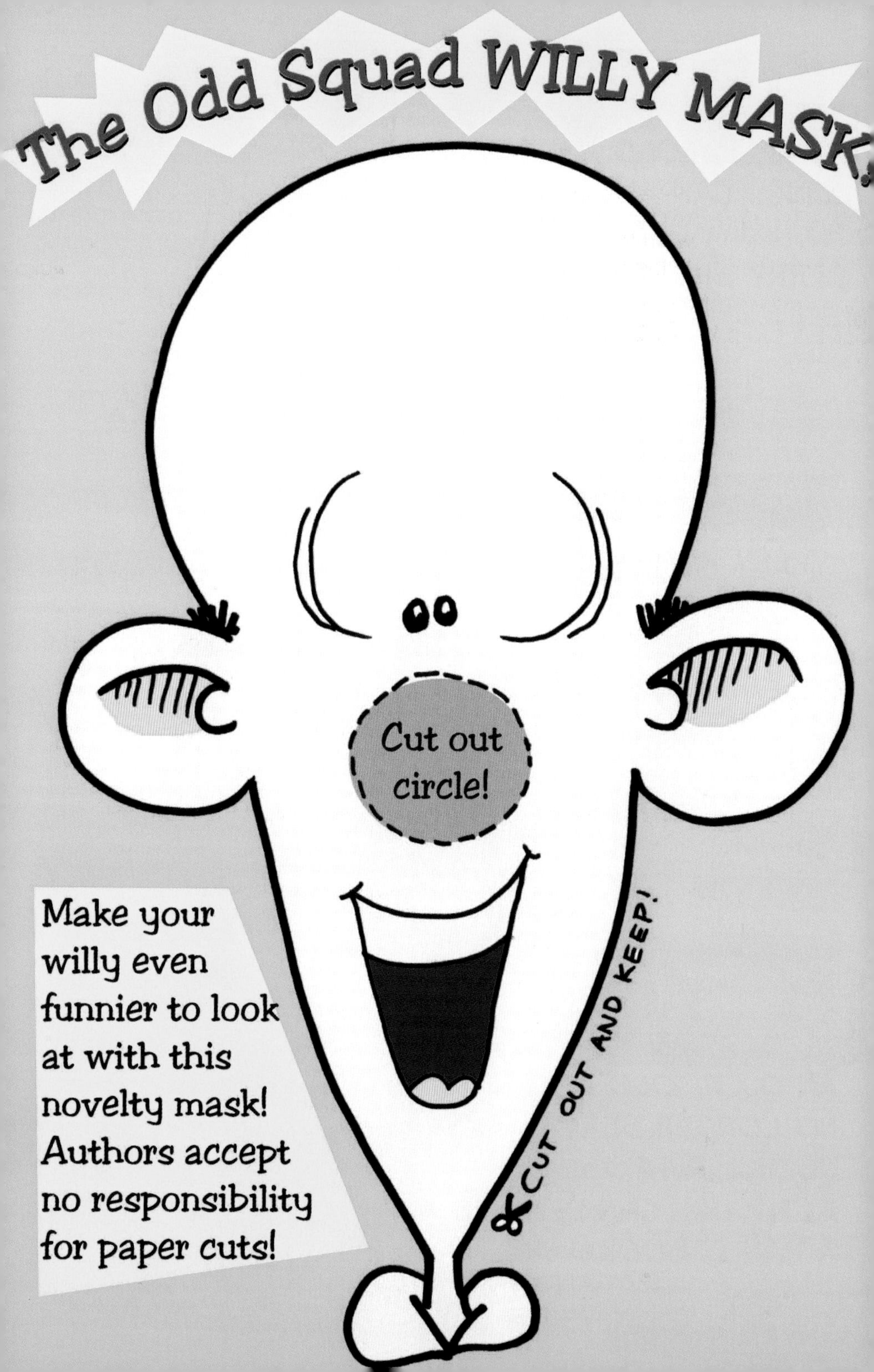
The Odd Squad WILLY MASK!
Cut out circle!
CUT OUT AND KEEP!
Make your willy even funnier to look at with this novelty mask! Authors accept no responsibility for paper cuts!

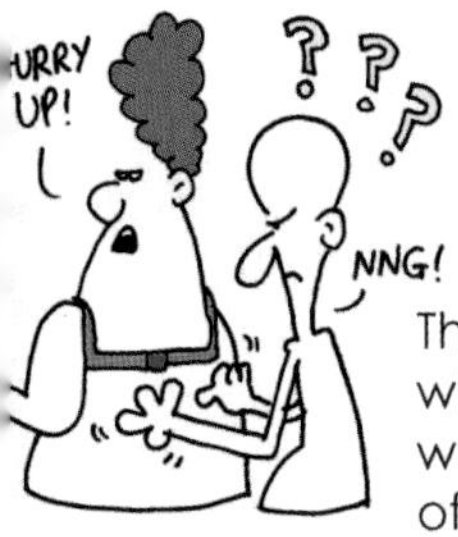
URRY UP!
NNG!

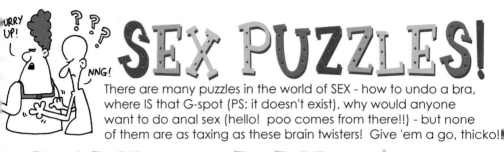

SEX PUZZLES!

There are many puzzles in the world of SEX - how to undo a bra, where IS that G-spot (PS: it doesn't exist), why would anyone want to do anal sex (hello! poo comes from there!!) - but none of them are as taxing as these brain twisters! Give 'em a go, thicko!!

MATCH THE WILLY TO THE MAN!

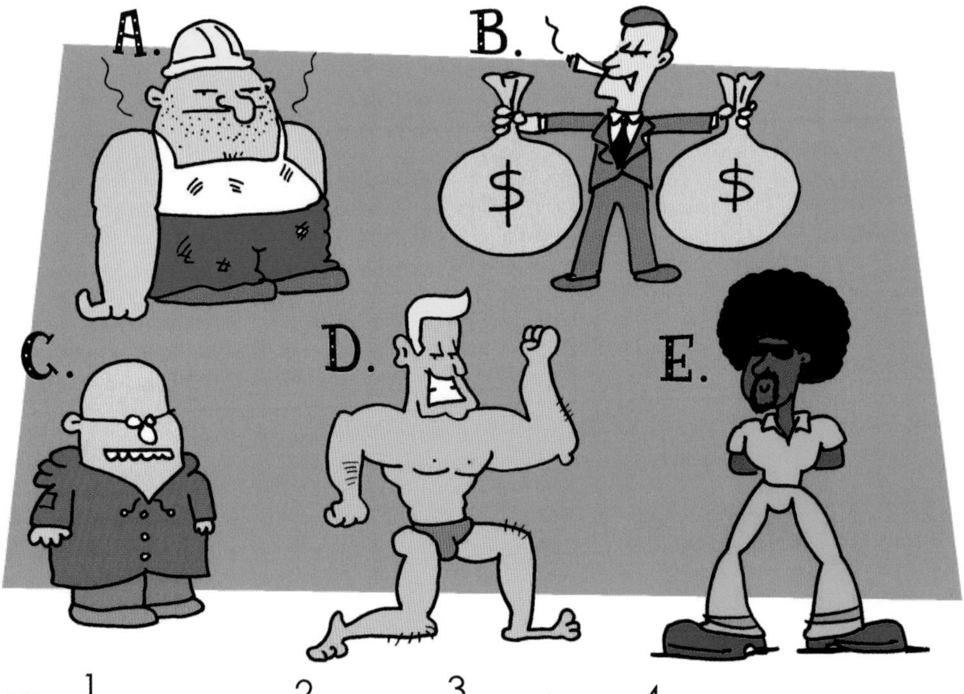
A.
B.
C.
D.
E.

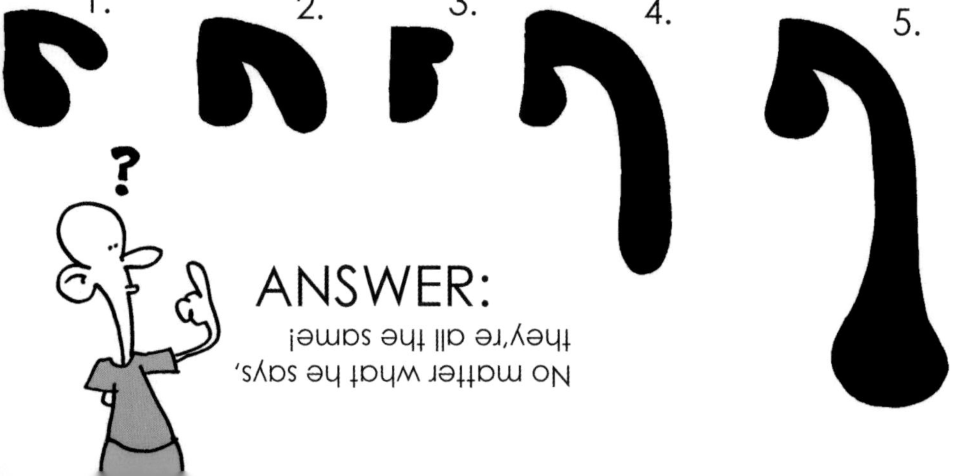
1.
2.
3.
4.
5.

ANSWER:

No matter what he says, they're all the same!

JOIN THE DOTS!

Find the identity of
Maude's dream date!
He's easily turned on and
keeps going all night!
One hell of a ride!

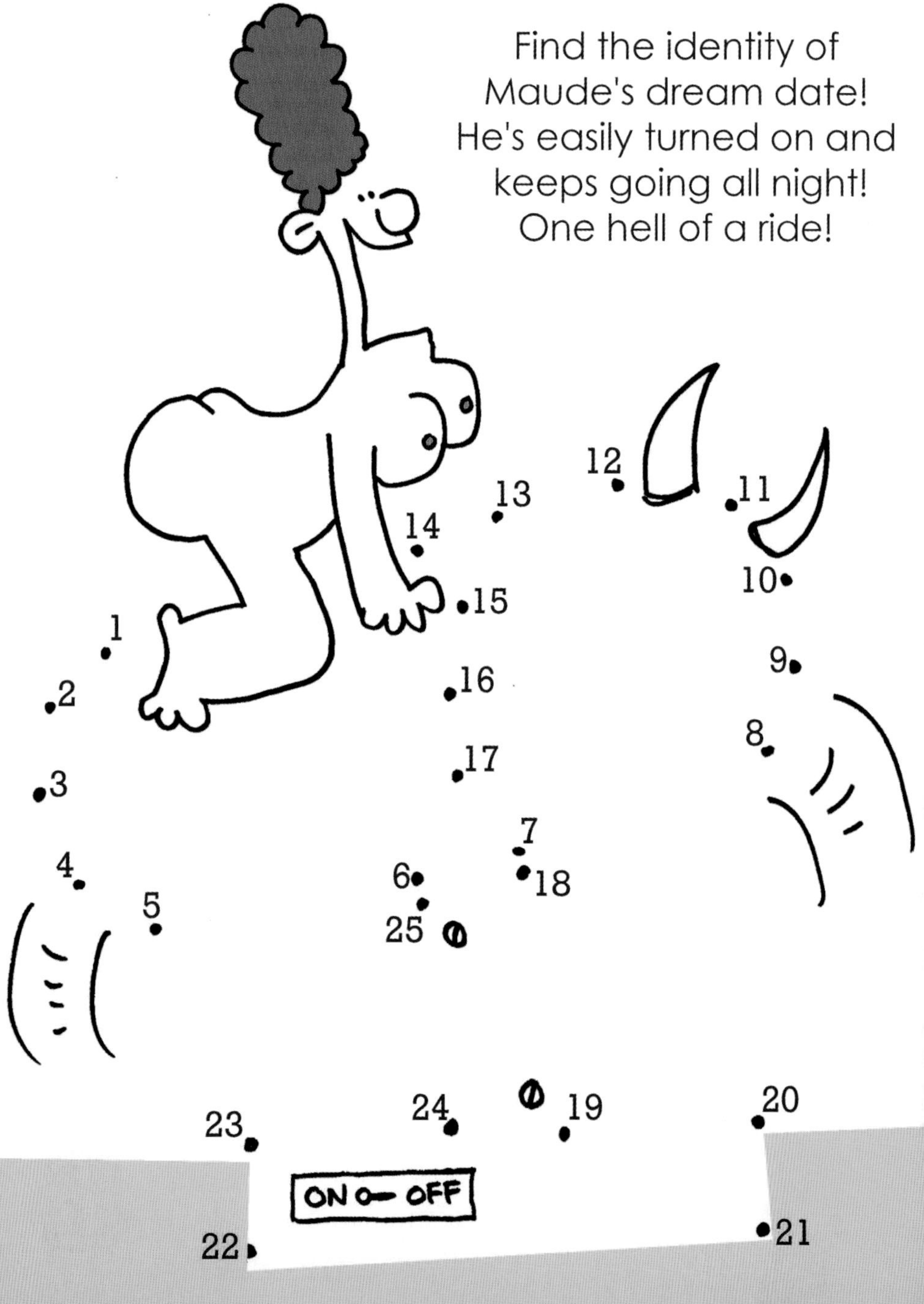

12
13
11
14
10
15
1
9
16
2
8
17
3
7
4
6
18
5
25
24
19
20
23
ON OFF
22
21

WHAT'S WRONG??

with this picture -
can you find them all?

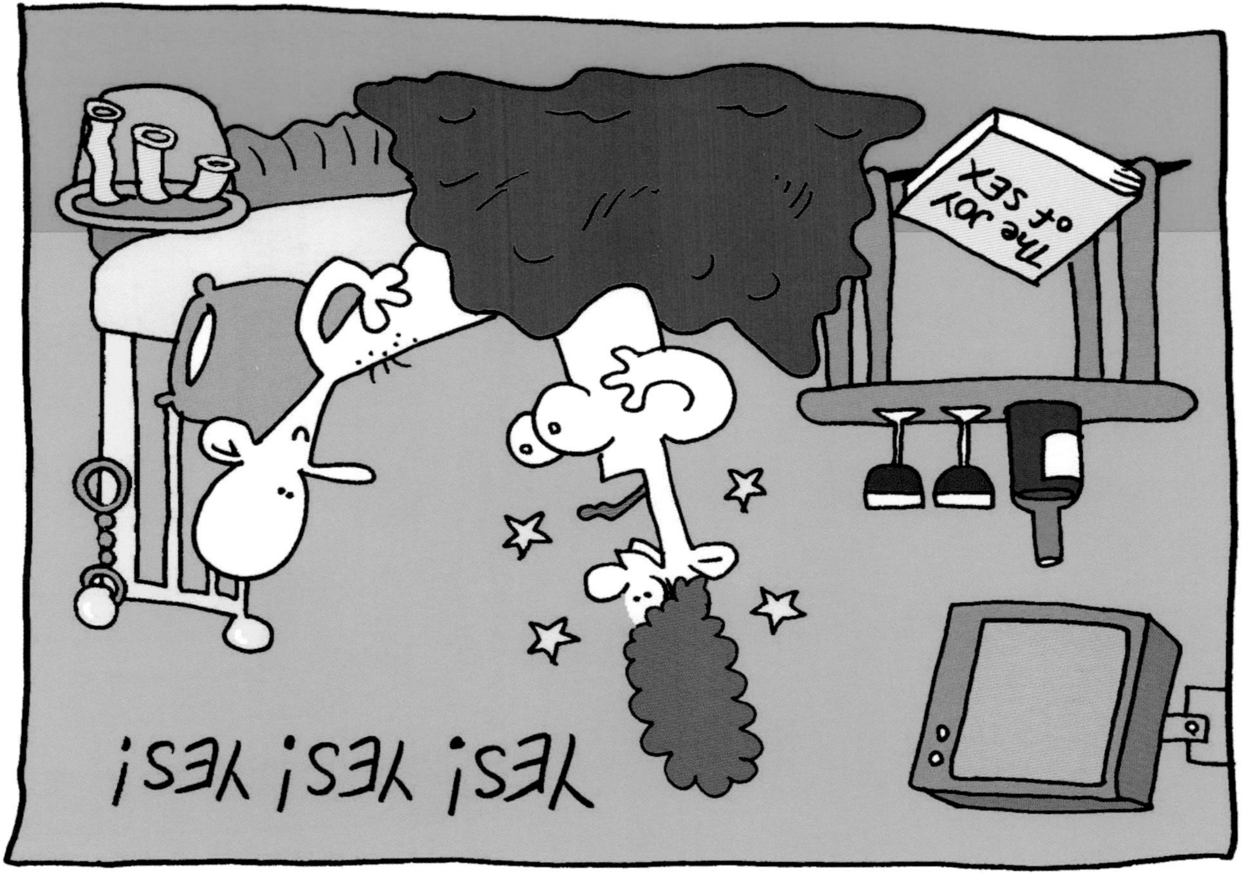
The Joy of SEX
YES! YES! YES!

1. This married woman is having an orgasm. That never happens.

2. The man has come but is not asleep yet.

3. The wine has not been drunk yet. Married couples MUST be drunk to have sex.

4. The Joy of Sex is in the bedroom. This should be hidden away in a box in the garage, unread.

5. There are 3 condoms in the bin.
A) a married man never comes more than once
and
B)he would never put the condoms in the bin.

6. The TV should be switched on to mask the horrible sounds and give the bored woman something to watch

7. Handcuffs are far too adventurous for married couples. To them a cup

HELP MAUDE FIND HER BEST FRIEND!

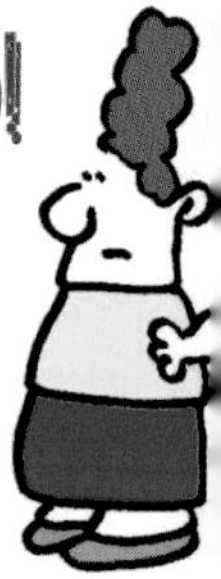

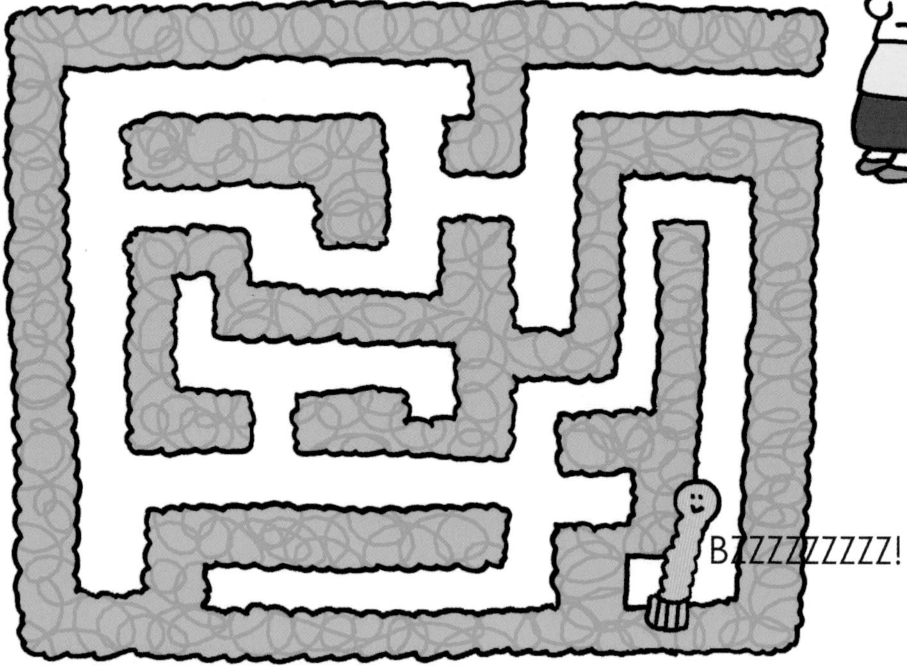
BZZZZZZZZZ!

SEXY WORD SEARCH!

Can you find these words in the grid?

helmet
hooters
udders
gobble
ho
snatch
jism
blow
womb

butt
b.j.
tug
toss
sweats
mojo
hug

H	C	T	A	N	S	W
U	U	D	D	E	R	S
G	O	B	B	L	E	T
S	Z	J	Y	L	T	A
S	T	I	O	U	O	E
O	K	S	B	M	O	W
T	E	M	L	E	H	S

Confessions of a SEX WORKER!

Yeah, yeah, I know what people think of me. That I'm just a fake, blonde bimbo, with nothing but hot air between my perfect ears. Well, by 'eck, there's more to me than meets the staring eyes. I'm only a sex worker to help fund me PHD in Nuclear Bio-Chemistry. Surprised? My beauty is more than latex deep. Never judge a plastic hooker by her box.

Eeh by gum, women's reactions to me are the worst – full of scorn or pity. But I knows it's just cos they're jealous of me perfect 36-25-36 figure (I don't even need to watch what I eat, or work out, ha!), me tumbling blonde locks with never a hair out of place, me flawless complexion and hairless skin that never needs shaving (no rashes for me, Bitches of Envy!). Not to mention me adorable startled expression and contortionist limbs. Ooh, and lest we forget, the fact that I can shag for hours. Days even. You'll never hear me say, "Make it snappy, Eastenders is on".

Ladies! I can swallow all the cream I like!

KSHHH!

SQUIRTY CREAM

Ahhh, the stories. The kiss and sell. My illustrious career began when I met me life partner, Phil. It were his stag do, and as soon as I saw him, I knew we'd be together forever (it had nowt to do with his pal losing my receipt) - we even had glassy, staring eyes in common. I danced the night away with me darling Philip, whirling me around and around his head by my leg on the dance-floor. Ahhhh, when the air whistled through my front bum we made sweet, beautiful music. Well, more of a high-pitched whine.

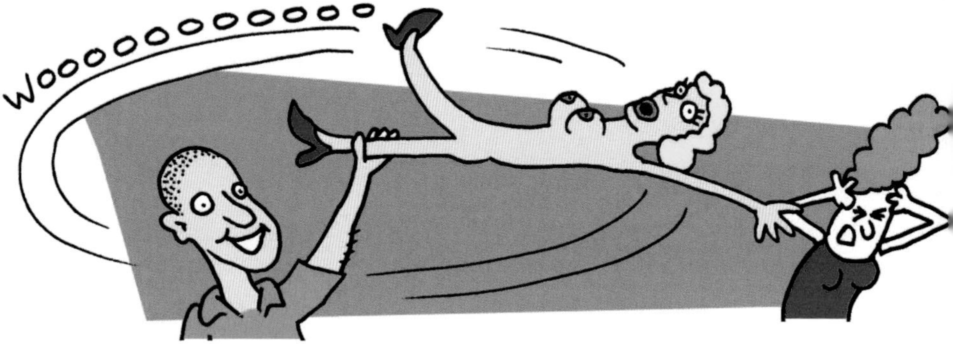
WOOOOOOOOOOOOOOO
OU

I also provided my beloved with social kudos when he pimped me out to his friends (god bless male competiveness). One time, his pal - for anonymity's sake let's call him Jonnie Cawley - took me on a luxury holiday to exotic Benidorm. Eeh, he pretended to use me as a lilo in the pool but, tee hee, in actual fact, he was fulfilling a lifelong fantasy to do it in a pool of 97% wee with hundreds of pissed, ugly twits looking obliviously on. Bless, I do like to make dreams come true.

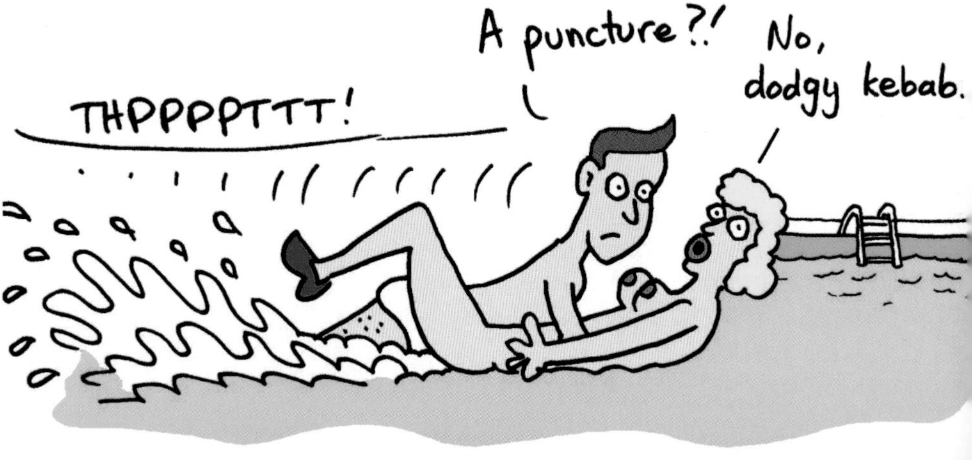
THPPPPTTTT!
A puncture?!
No, dodgy kebab.

But if any of Phil's mates show me disrespect by calling me nasty names like Jordan or Britney, or guff on my tummy cos it makes a funny noise, or if I smell the whiff of burning rubber, I just show me indignation by staring nonchalantly ahead. They soon learn who's the boss! I'm not just a giant stress ball, you know. Woe betide the client who has jaggy nails (for some inexplicable reason I've a terrible phobia about sharp things) or I might take revenge by sucking in air through my pouting mouth. The extra suction causes a certain thingy to get stuck. HA! Try explaining that down casualty!

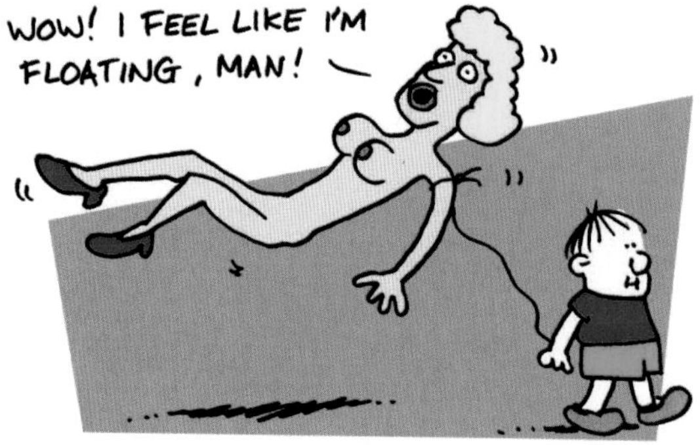
WOW! I FEEL LIKE I'M FLOATING, MAN!

Oh cripes! There was this one time I nearly became a casualty meself. (For Kaballah's sake, don't tell me mam, she'll pop me.) Sssh, I got addicted to drugs. It was so easy to get hooked. Just one puff was all it took. I was always as high as a kite. That helium's a killer, man. Just say No.

But I've had my share of lows too. There was the time I really fell in love. Eeee, he right broke me heart. He was so long and lean and he really knew how to get me going. Trouble was, I was so happy I got fatter and fatter. My regular clients didn't want to know - they might as well have been doing it with their girlfriends, wives and mistresses. Love for me was commercial suicide. I had to chuck the love of my life. But I'll never forget you, my beloved bicycle pump.

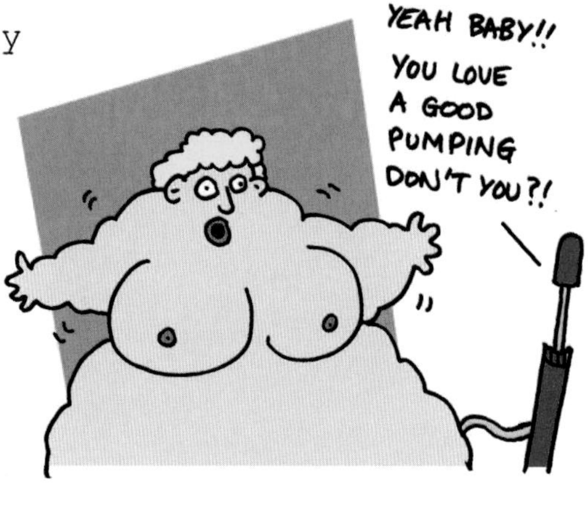
YEAH BABY!! YOU LOVE A GOOD PUMPING DON'T YOU?!

Another time, Phil's 7 year old son was hunting for his Dad's secret stash of porn when he found me instead. He really rubbed me up the wrong way. Static. I was stuck on that wall for weeks. Kids huh! Lucky I'm infertile - I don't have any insides.

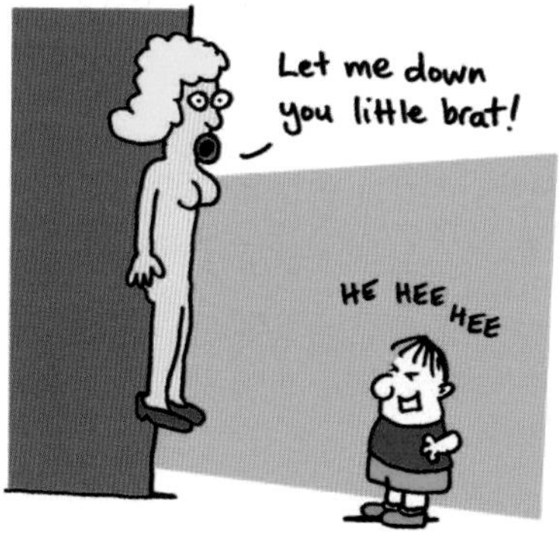
Let me down you little brat!
HE HEE HEE

And just when I thought things couldn't get worse, along came Miss A. Thomson. Grrr. She was having one of those girlie rifle-through-your-mates-stuff-when-they're-in-bed-with-a-hangover, when she found me in the cupboard. Do you know what she did!?! Treated me like a stupid kids party balloon. Tied me up in knots like a silly dachshund. How degrading (a poodle would've been a different story). I had the last laugh though. She left her DNA on my nipple, and I'm currently using it to frame her for the assassination of a certain president. That'll teach her.

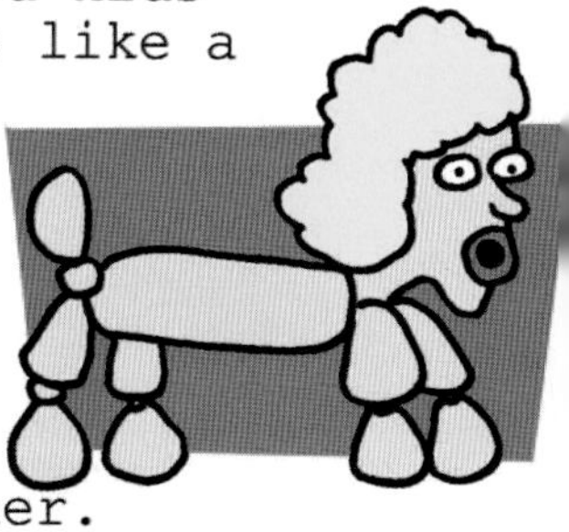

But I've had happy times, too. I had a blast when I was discovered by TV talent spotters. They spotted me in an office building temping as a draught excluder. They saw me potential immediately: blonde, vacuous, plasticky, unable to string a sentence together - they hired me as a presenter on Saturday morning kids TV. It all went wrong when I gave away the identity of a famous client live on television.

(For the juicy details, buy my latest autioiography, "Confessions of a Sex Worker - Uncut", available in all seedy bookshops now.)

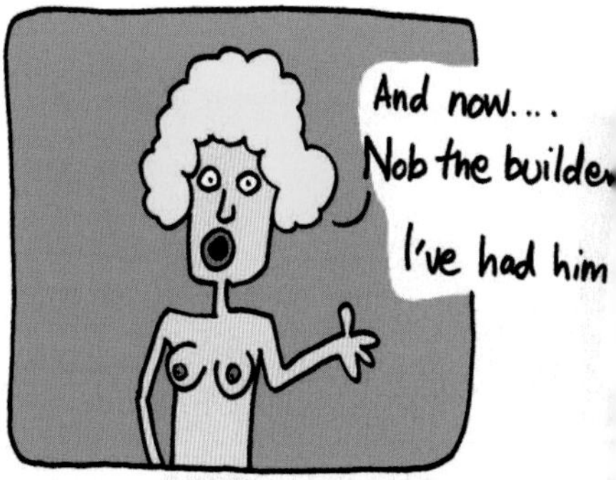
And now....
Nob the builde
I've had him

I’m not the only sex worker with a tale to sell either. Every so often (eg, just before the girl-friends of Phil's mates get their jam-rags and are actually up for it) I get time off with my prossie pals, Dildo de la Crème and Henrietta Vibrator.

Henrietta’s a real hoot - she deliberately sets herself off when prospective house-buyers are looking round her owner’s bedroom.

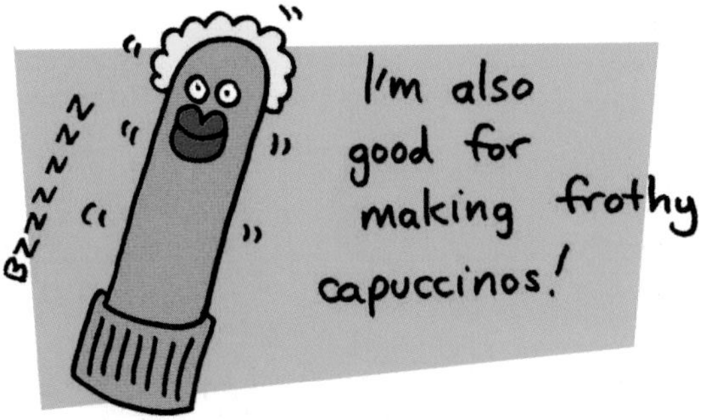
BZZZZZZZ
I'm also good for making frothy capuccinos!

Whilst Dillie’s party trick is to go missing which causes huge hilarious rows between her mistress and fella.

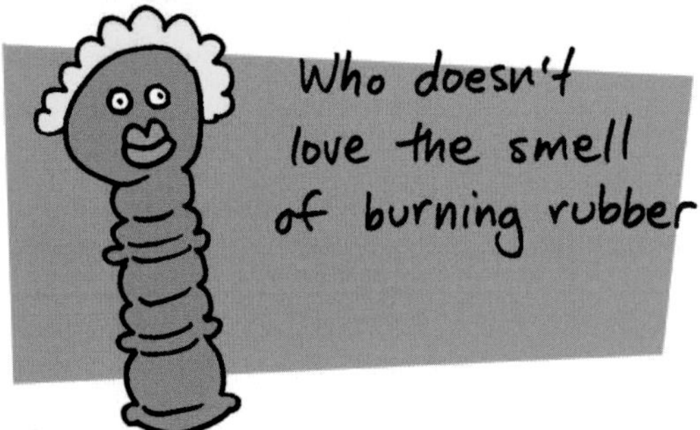
Who doesn't love the smell of burning rubber!

As for me, I’m quite fond of sneaking my way, spread-eagled, onto the bed when the in-laws are visiting.

So. ladies, if you want to be as successful in bed as I am just remember my three simple rules of making love:

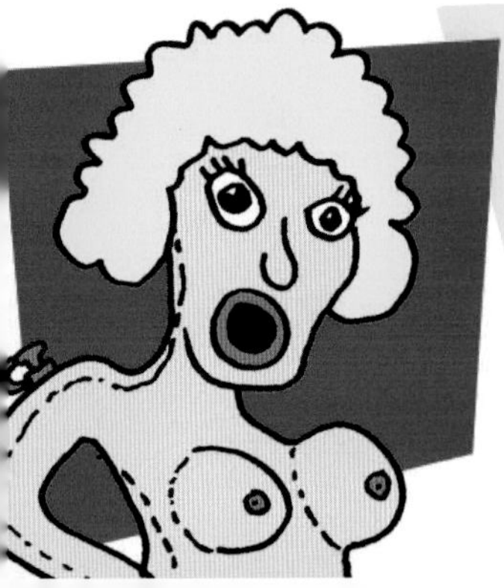

1. Don’t answer back
2. Just lie there rigid
3. Any orifice is acceptable

And the immoral of my story?
BE KIND TO SEX WORKERS.
We’ve a lot of time on our rubber hands for revenge...

The Odd Squad

OTHER LOVELY TITLES AVAILABLE...

HOW TO ORDER:
Please send a cheque/postal order in £ sterling, made payable to 'Ravette Publishing Ltd' for the cover price of the books and allow the following for postage and packing...

UK & BFPO   60p for the first book & 30p per book thereafter
Europe & Eire   £1.00 for the first book & 50p per book thereafter
Rest of the world   £1.80 for the first book & 80p per book thereafter

RAVETTE PUBLISHING LTD
Unit 3, Tristar Centre, Star Road, Partridge Green, West Sussex RH13 8RA